1980s Project Studies/Council on Foreign Relations

STUDIES AVAILABLE

CONTROLLING FUTURE ARMS TRADE
Studies by Anne Hessing Cahn and Joseph J. Kruzel, by Peter M. Dawkins, and by Jacques Huntzinger

DIVERSITY AND DEVELOPMENT IN SOUTHEAST ASIA:
The Coming Decade
Studies by Guy J. Pauker, Frank H. Golay, and Cynthia H. Enloe

NUCLEAR WEAPONS AND WORLD POLITICS:
Alternatives for the Future
Studies by David C. Gompert, Michael Mandelbaum, Richard L. Garwin, and John H. Barton

CHINA'S FUTURE:
Foreign Policy and Economic Development in the Post-Mao Era
Studies by Allen S. Whiting and by Robert F. Dernberger

ALTERNATIVES TO MONETARY DISORDER
Studies by Fred Hirsch and Michael W. Doyle and by Edward L. Morse

NUCLEAR PROLIFERATION:
Motivations, Capabilities, and Strategies for Control
Studies by Ted Greenwood and by Harold A. Feiveson and Theodore B. Taylor

INTERNATIONAL DISASTER RELIEF:
Toward a Responsive System
Stephen Green

STUDIES FORTHCOMING

Some 20 additional volumes of the 1980s Project work will be appearing in the course of the next year or two. Most will contain independent but related studies concerning issues of potentially great importance in the next decade and beyond, such as resource management, terrorism, and relations between the developing and developed societies, among many others. Additionally, a number of volumes will be devoted to particular regions of the world, concentrating especially on political and economic development trends outside the industrialized West.

Controlling Future Arms Trade

ANNE HESSING CAHN

and JOSEPH J. KRUZEL

PETER M. DAWKINS

JACQUES HUNTZINGER

Introduction by David C. Gompert
and Alexander R. Vershbow

1980s Project/Council on Foreign Relations

McGRAW-HILL BOOK COMPANY

New York   St. Louis   San Francisco
Auckland   Bogotá   Düsseldorf   Johannesburg   London   Madrid
Mexico   Montreal   New Delhi   Panama   Paris   São Paulo
Singapore   Sydney   Tokyo   Toronto

Tallahassee, Florida

The Council on Foreign Relations, Inc. is a nonprofit and nonpartisan organization devoted to promoting improved understanding of international affairs through the free exchange of ideas. Its membership of about 1,700 persons throughout the United States is made up of individuals with special interest and experience in international affairs. The Council has no affiliation with and receives no funding from the United States government.

The Council publishes the quarterly journal *Foreign Affairs* and, from time to time, books and monographs which in the judgment of the Council's Committee on Studies are responsible treatments of significant international topics worthy of presentation to the public. The 1980s Project is a research effort of the Council; as such, 1980s Project Studies have been similarly reviewed through procedures of the Committee on Studies. As in the case of all Council publications, statements of fact and expressions of opinion contained in 1980s Project Studies are the sole responsibility of their authors.

The editor of this book was Alexander R. Vershbow for the Council on Foreign Relations. Thomas Quinn and Michael Hennelly were the editors for McGraw-Hill Book Company. Christopher Simon was the designer. Teresa Leaden supervised the production. This book was set in Times Roman by Creative Book Services, Inc.
Printed and bound by R. R. Donnelley & Sons.

Library of Congress Cataloging in Publication Data
Main entry under title:
Controlling future arms trade.
(1980s project/Council on Foreign Relations)
Bibliography: p.
Includes index.
1. Munitions—Addresses, essays, lectures.
2. Disarmament—Addresses, essays, lectures.
I. Cahn, Anne H. II. Series: Council on Foreign
Relations. 1980s project—Council on Foreign Relations.
HD9743.A2C57   382'.45'6234   77-22039
ISBN 0-07-009589-2
ISBN 0-07-009590-6 pbk.

1 2 3 4 5 6 7 8 9 R R D R R D 7 0 9 8 7

Contents

Foreword: The 1980s Project

The studies in this volume analyze and prescribe measures to curb the vast international trade in military weapons, which has grown so much in recent years and which now consumes a large proportion of the resources of many nations. They are part of a stream of studies to be produced in the course of the 1980s Project of the Council on Foreign Relations, each of which analyzes an issue or set of issues likely to be of international concern during the next 10 to 20 years. The ambitious purpose of the 1980s Project is to examine important political and economic problems not only individually but in relationship to one another. Some studies or books produced by the Project will primarily emphasize the interrelationship of issues. In the case of other, more specifically focused studies, a considerable effort has been made to write, review, and criticize them in the context of more general Project work. Each Project study is thus capable of standing on its own; at the same time it has been shaped by a broader perspective.

The 1980s Project had its origins in the widely held recognition that many of the assumptions, policies, and institutions that have characterized international relations during the past 30 years are inadequate to the demands of today and the foreseeable demands of the period between now and 1990 or so. Over the course of the next decade, substantial adaptation of institutions and behavior will be needed to respond to the changed circumstances of the 1980s and beyond. The Project seeks to identify those future conditions and the kinds of adaptation they might require. It is not the Project's purpose to arrive at a single or exclusive set of goals. Nor does it focus upon the foreign policy or national interests of the United States alone. Instead, it seeks to identify goals that are compatible with the perceived interests of most states, despite differences in ideology and in level of economic development.

The published products of the Project are aimed at a broad readership, including policy makers and potential policy makers and those who would influence the policy-making process, but are confined to no single nation or region. The authors of Project studies were therefore asked to remain mindful of interests broader than those of any one society and to take fully into account the likely realities of domestic politics in the principal societies involved. All those who have worked in the Project, however, have tried not to be captives of the status quo; they have sought to question the inevitability of existing patterns of thought and behavior that restrain desirable change and to look for ways in which those patterns might in time be altered or their consequences mitigated.

The 1980s Project is at once a series of separate attacks upon a number of urgent and potentially urgent international problems and also a collective effort, involving a substantial number of persons in the United States and abroad, to bring those separate approaches to bear upon one another and to suggest the kinds of choices that might be made among them. The Project involves more than 300 participants. A small central staff and a steering Coordinating Group have worked to define the questions and to assess the compatibility of policy prescriptions. Nearly 100 authors, from more than a dozen countries, have been at work on separate studies. Ten working groups of specialists and generalists have been convened to subject the Project's studies to critical scrutiny and to help in the process of identifying interrelationships among them.

The 1980s Project is the largest single research and studies effort the Council on Foreign Relations has undertaken in its 55-year history, comparable in conception only to a major study of the postwar world, the War and Peace Studies, undertaken by the Council during the Second World War. At that time, the impetus to the effort was the discontinuity caused by worldwide conflict and the visible and inescapable need to rethink, replace, and supplement many of the features of the international system that had prevailed before the war. The discontinuities in today's world are less obvious and, even when occasionally quite visible—as in the abandonment of gold convertibility and fixed monetary parities—only briefly command the spotlight of public attention. That new institutions and patterns of behavior are needed in many areas is widely acknowledged, but the sense of need is less urgent—existing institutions have not for the most part dramatically failed and collapsed. The tendency, therefore, is to make do with outmoded arrangements and to improvise rather than to undertake a basic analysis of the problems that lie before us and of the demands that those problems will place upon all nations.

The 1980s Project is based upon the belief that serious effort and integrated forethought can contribute—indeed, are indispensable—to progress in the next decade toward a more humane, peaceful, productive, and just world. And it rests upon the hope that participants in its deliberations and readers of Project publications—whether or not they agree with an author's point of view—may be helped to think more informedly about the opportunities and the dangers that lie ahead and the consequences of various possible courses of future action.

The 1980s Project has been made possible by generous grants from the Ford Foundation, the Lilly Endowment, the Andrew W. Mellon Foundation, the Rockefeller Foundation, and the German Marshall Fund of the United States. Neither the Council on Foreign Relations nor any of those foundations is responsible for statements of fact and expressions of opinion contained in publications of the 1980s Project; they are the sole responsibility of the individual authors under whose names they appear. But the Council on Foreign Relations and the staff of the 1980s Project take great pleasure in placing those publications before a wide readership both in the United States and abroad.

Edward L. Morse and Richard H. Ullman

ix

1980s PROJECT WORKING GROUPS

During 1975 and 1976, ten Working Groups met to explore major international issues and to subject initial drafts of 1980s Project studies to critical review. Those who chaired Project Working Groups were:

Cyrus R. Vance, Working Group on Nuclear Weapons and Other Weapons of Mass Destruction

Leslie H. Gelb, Working Group on Armed Conflict

Roger Fisher, Working Group on Transnational Violence and Subversion

Rev. Theodore M. Hesburgh, Working Group on Human Rights

Joseph S. Nye, Jr., Working Group on the Political Economy of North-South Relations

Harold Van B. Cleveland, Working Group on Macroeconomic Policies and International Monetary Relations

Lawrence C. McQuade, Working Group on Principles of International Trade

William Diebold, Jr., Working Group on Multinational Enterprises

Eugene B. Skolnikoff, Working Group on the Environment, the Global Commons, and Economic Growth

Miriam Camps, Working Group on Industrial Policy

1980s PROJECT STAFF

Persons who have held senior professional positions on the staff of the 1980s Project for all or part of its duration are:

Miriam Camps	*Catherine Gwin*
William Diebold, Jr.	*Roger D. Hansen*
Tom J. Farer	*Edward L. Morse*
David C. Gompert	*Richard H. Ullman*

Richard H. Ullman was Director of the 1980s Project from its inception in 1974 until July 1977, when he became Chairman of the Project Coordinating Group. At that time, Edward L. Morse became Executive Director of the Project.

Introduction: Controlling Arms Trade

David C. Gompert and Alexander R. Vershbow

The global trade in conventional armaments has become a burning political issue in recent years, owing primarily to the dramatic increase in the volume of the international market since the early 1970s. Excoriation and pontification concerning this upsurge in the "death business" has intensified. The Carter Administration has identified limiting international arms transfers as a high-priority foreign policy objective. Moreover, by most estimates, the phenomenon will not be short-lived. Though the volume of arms trade may contract somewhat following the current boom, arms transfers will remain a significant international activity at least well into the next decade. The possibility of control is thus of both immediate and long-term interest.

But what does it mean to "control" international arms traffic? Is the goal to reduce the quantities of arms sold or given as aid, to discriminate among those who want arms, to restrict the types of arms that may be traded, to set and enforce conditions on how the arms may be used, or a combination of these pursuits? It is difficult to get agreement among individuals, let alone among governments, as to the nature of the arms trade "problem" or even whether there is a problem. The purpose of this 1980s Project volume is to stimulate public discussion of transfers of

NOTE: This essay was written before David C. Gompert and Alexander R. Vershbow entered government service. The views expressed are those of the authors and do not necessarily reflect the views of the United States government or any of its agencies or departments.

1

non-nuclear arms as a matter of long-term international concern rather than as a current controversy over who should get how many of what sort of weapons from whom. The volume has two concrete objectives: to clarify the nature of the arms trade problem as projected into the coming decade and to offer several realistic international approaches to dealing with it.[1]

Specifically, Anne Cahn and Joseph Kruzel attempt to project the major dimensions of arms trade well into the next decade. Peter Dawkins offers some recommendations on how the nations that export arms might cooperate to restrict the quantities, types, destinations, and uses of their exported weapons. Jacques Huntzinger provides several models by which nations that import arms might organize regionally to institute restraint. Simply put, Cahn and Kruzel analyze the problem, Dawkins addresses the prospects for controlling supply, and Huntzinger deals with curbing demand. This introductory essay is intended to set the issue of conventional arms trade in a somewhat larger context, to illuminate important analytical and normative differences among the essays that follow, and to suggest how some of the prescriptions made in the essays might be fit together in the form of cooperative importer-exporter efforts to control the market and its effects.

There are many ways of viewing arms trade. At one extreme is the argument—or intuitive assumption—that exports of arms, by sales or as aid, are inherently harmful, inasmuch as without arms wars are impractical or at least not very destructive. The greater the volume of traffic, according to this line of reasoning, the more likely—and potentially more violent—are wars among arms recipients. At the opposite extreme is the argument that it is the sovereign prerogative of every state to determine its own security needs and to acquire whatever weapons it can afford to satisfy those needs; it is equally within the rights of states that are blessed with the resources to manufacture arms to sell or give them to those willing to pay the economic and/or political price. Accord-

---

[1] This volume deals only with *non-nuclear*, or ''conventional,'' arms. The issue of the spread of *nuclear* weapons is dealt with in another 1980s Project book, by Ted Greenwood, Harold A. Feiveson and Theodore B. Taylor, *Nuclear Proliferation: Motivations, Capabilities, and Strategies for Control*, McGraw-Hill, New York, 1977.

ing to this view, arms transfers should be treated as just another aspect of international intercourse. The operation of the market brings benefit to buyer and seller alike; what is good for each who chooses to participate in the market cannot be bad in the aggregate.

Yet another—and more fruitful—way of approaching the issue of arms trade is to view it both as a *systemic* phenomenon, in which the implements of war and power are spreading from the industrialized world into the developing world, and as a series of individual transactions or national policies, each with particular *situational* motivations and implications involving relations between suppliers and recipients and between recipients and their neighbors. The essays that follow develop this mode of analysis. Each of the authors recognizes that since most of the arms to be transferred in the next decade will be flowing into the developing world, where regional and local security concerns are paramount, the best way to assess the situational hazards and benefits of arms transfers is through examination of their effects on regional political-military patterns.

Many critics of today's arms trade argue that transfers usually feed local arms races, heighten regional tensions, and jeopardize regional power equilibriums, thereby raising the risks of local war. They maintain that the purchase of arms from abroad by less developed states is a tragic waste of scarce resources, aggravating poverty within the developing societies and stifling motives toward generosity among publics—and their elected representatives—in the advanced industrialized societies.

Opponents of this view stress that arms transfers can help correct regional power imbalances by shoring up the weaker states threatened by self-styled or foreign-backed regional bullies, or by equipping states within the developing world to resist intervention and intimidation by external powers, especially those most capable of and prone toward intervention—the United States and the Soviet Union. These skeptics of the desirability of control contend that the purchase of arms by developing countries, in giving them a strong defense capability—a symbol, if not a prerequisite, of national sovereignty—enhances national self-esteem, diplomatic flexibility, and, consequently, prospects for

3

development, while the most plausible alternative to arms trade, indigenous military production, is a less efficient and potentially more hazardous way of satisfying the specific demands for arms throughout the developing world. What may appear to outsiders to be an excessive demand for arms, leading to muscle-boundness if the demand is met, may be seen in individual Third World capitals as an effort to guarantee national security—hardly a sinister or misguided objective when it is held by leaders of Western, industrialized countries in the light of their *own* national military needs and objectives, the importance of which they would not want outsiders to decide.

World opinion is no less divided on the meaning of arms trade as a systemic phenomenon. Many observers diagnose the proliferation of conventional weapons—and the know-how to maintain, reproduce, and use them—as an important element of a general diffusion of power from the industrialized core to the developing periphery. Paralleling the spread of nuclear weapons, accelerated by the fragmentation of cold war global alliance systems and the erosion of the political authority of the great and once-great powers, financed by the shift of economic power as epitomized by the rise of the oil producers, arms transfers may be seen both as a reflection of and as a mechanism for greater equalization between North and South. Many who favor this general systemic trend see efforts by producers to restrict the spread of arms—while they themselves maintain massive arsenals—as motivated not by altruistic concerns for regional security in the Third World but by a self-interested desire to retard the seepage of power.

Yet another, less sanguine view—one emphasized in Soviet analyses (when the arms sales being criticized are Western) and echoed by neo-Marxists in Western and in Third World countries—sees arms transfers as an increasingly important strand in a web of policies, activities, and relationships by which the rich and powerful perpetuate their control over dependent nations. The "new imperialism" has abandoned the clumsy, costly tools of formal colonialism, troop presence, and intervention in favor of more subtle—not to mention lucrative—instruments: exploitative trade, manipulative and extractive investment, and in the security area, dependency-creating arms commerce and investment (the latter known euphemistically as

4

co-production) between industrialized patrons and underdeveloped clients. By keeping puppets in power, by distorting the military policies of developing states to conform with the needs of superpower geostrategic competition, and by preempting indigenous production and self-reliance in the Third World, arms trade facilitates the continuation of an inequitable international system, camouflaged by the myth of a diffusion of power. Restrictions on arms trade, in this radical perspective, will be resisted by those who appreciate the uses of dependency.

These are sweeping explanations—and explanations which sweep away discordant facts. They are noted here not because they are represented in this volume but because they form a significant part of the intellectual and political background against which discussion of the complex phenomena of arms trade takes place. Most knowledgeable observers—and the authors of the studies which follow—appreciate the need for "mixed models" of analysis and prescription at both the situational and the systemic levels. There would appear to be a need for *some* control. And there would appear to be potential sources of support for some control across a wide range of viewpoints falling between the extremes just identified. Indeed, control that is not worked out among various interests may be of little utility and durability. Although the 1980s Project asked Dawkins and Huntzinger to approach the problem from opposite directions—Dawkins making a case for supplier restraint, Huntzinger presenting an advocate's brief for restraints by arms recipients—they both recognize the need for cooperation between exporters and importers as well as among exporters and among importers. In the remaining pages of this introduction, following some observations on the context of arms transfers in the 1980s and on the costs of control, we will suggest how the ideas presented in the subsequent essays might help enable exporters and importers (or, if you like, clients and patrons, or crumbling core and challenging periphery) to find common ground and common benefit through control.

THE CONTEXT OF ARMS TRADE IN THE 1980s

The issue of conventional arms trade lies at the intersection of the two dominant axes of contemporary world politics: the geostrategic contest between East and West and the political-economic relationship between the developed North and the developing South. Analyzing arms trade as it is likely to develop in the 1980s requires some effort at understanding how these two relationships are likely to evolve and interact.

The states of the developing world are loosening their bonds of alignment with one or the other pole of strategic power.[2] Yet East-West—specifically, Soviet-American—competition in the Third World will persist. Notwithstanding such developments as the growth of "Eurocommunism," renewed pressures for greater diversity in Eastern Europe, and increased multipolarity of East Asian international politics, these traditional arenas of the East-West tug-of-war have become and will likely remain quite stable. Washington and Moscow both accept the basic status quo in Europe and the Far East or at least recognize that the risks of trying to effect revisions are prohibitively high. But the days of Soviet-American competition have not passed with the advent of détente. The fluid politics outside the traditional arenas present an inviting set of opportunities and challenges to the two global powers, which may lead them increasingly to view the Third World as a natural, and perhaps unavoidable, theater for East-West political competition.

Arms transfers are and will likely remain a key element of this competition. That arms are now sold far more than given as grant aid hardly ensures that commercial considerations will typically prevail over calculations of political gain and loss in shaping arms transfer policy in Moscow and Washington. Each superpower will continue to enjoy influence and special prerogatives where it is the main supplier of arms. That the arms are now purchased obviously does not mean that recipients need them less; if anything, it suggests that they may be even more critically needed, at least in the eyes of the recipients, than in the days when they could be had for free.

Moreover, with the rise in the technological sophistication of the weapons being transferred in recent years, recipients have

[2]While such alignments have in general been more extensive and more formal on the Western side, clients and allies of the Soviet Union are also attempting to exercise greater freedom to maneuver internationally.

become increasingly dependent on technical support services (e.g., spare parts) and personnel from the supplier country to maintain the advanced systems and to ensure adequate training for their use. Such dependence of course limits the freedom of recipients to change suppliers, to play off one supplier against another, and to resist the efforts of exporters to place conditions on or extract political returns from particular arms transactions and long-term arms transfer relationships.[3] Moreover, with the superpowers (especially the United States) becoming increasingly constrained from employing other instruments of power—intervention, standing military presence, and the use of Third World proxies to exert pressure indirectly against the rival superpower at the local level—in Third World contests, the use of arms transfers to strengthen and influence clients may become more vital than ever to the superpowers' international strategies.

But as Cahn and Kruzel argue, it would be a mistake to look only, or even primarily, at the modes and motives of global geostrategic competition in attempting to project the arms trade phenomenon into the 1980s. Noting that patron-client arms relationships often fail to earn significant political dividends for the patron (the Soviet experience in Egypt from 1956 to 1972 being the classic example) and also that economic power has shifted from North to South, they see increasing "commercialization" of the world's arms traffic.

North-South economics more than East-West politics will decide the directions, composition, and volume of armaments flow. The pattern of transfers in the 1980s, Cahn and Kruzel predict, will conform less and less to the division of influence between East and West; the Soviets and Americans will increasingly sell arms to each other's clients, while the clients will feel more free to bargain between East and West for the better deal. With the

---

[3] It is possible, however, that this trend toward increasing dependence on suppliers might be at least partially reversed in the 1980s if, as Cahn and Kruzel suggest, future weapons systems, while more sophisticated, also prove to be simpler to operate and maintain. Yet while dependence may be reduced for such smaller weapons, the problem of securing easily integrated follow-on systems, spare parts, and other support for major weapons systems (combat aircraft, tanks and other vehicles, helicopters) will discourage most arms recipients from becoming too fickle in their choice of suppliers.

United States facing at least another decade of massive dependence on foreign oil and consequent balance-of-payments problems, and with the Soviet Union beset by an apparently long-term poverty of hard currency, market forces will often prevail over political constraints in deciding who should and should not have purchasing access to how much of the superpowers' conventional arsenals. Moreover, the existence of other Northern arms exporters,[4] for whom East-West strategic competition is at most a secondary motive for selling arms, means even greater latitude for arms recipients in choosing among exporters.

As Cahn and Kruzel see it, the arms market is thus becoming a buyers' market. The sellers are under great pressure to reduce balance-of-payments deficits and to support national arms industries by maximizing sales; they are becoming less discriminating in their choice of arms-trading partners; they are selling better, newer weapons; they are less able to insist on restrictions on how the arms are to be used; they are less able to manipulate arms relationships for political ends; and they can no longer count on the fidelity of buyers to the political alignments and objectives that structure East-West relations. At the same time, the buyers are finding advanced weaponry more affordable and no longer have to satisfy themselves with obsolescent, "surplus" material; they are more resistant than ever to efforts by suppliers to use arms relationships for political manipulation; and some are beginning to reach a level of industrial development at which they can turn to domestic production of reasonably sophisticated weapons should they become dissatisfied with dependence on the international market.

The shifting currents of the North-South relationship have also created a new political incentive for the industrialized states to market their arms. As new sources of political-economic power—especially major producers of oil and other raw materials—emerge in the Third World, their potential for disrupting economic conditions among and within the industrialized states is inducing the latter to try to draw the former into closer harmony with Northern—especially Western—activities and in-

[4]For example, Britain, France, Sweden, and, though far from autonomous in its arms transfer policy because of its status as a Soviet client, Czechoslovakia.

terests.[5] Conventional weapons are often an important item in a package of political, economic, and technological relationships being offered by individual industrialized states not just to lure key developing states away from the strategic adversary but also to foster moderation among the recipients themselves.

It is impossible now to predict whether the East-West or the North-South axis of world arms trade will be dominant in the 1980s or how each axis will evolve. The more troubled East-West relations are, the more difficult it may be for the suppliers (especially the two superpowers) to identify common interests in restricting supplies. The more conflictual North-South political-economic relations are, the harder it may be for suppliers and recipients to act cooperatively to control arms trade on a bilateral or multilateral basis. That these relationships will remain crucial and complex suggests that neither collaboration among the exporters nor cooperation between exporters and importers will suffice; rather, both will be needed in order to control the market.

But again we face the question, Why control the market? Neither East-West nor North-South considerations provide a satisfactory answer. The need to control world arms trade becomes apparent only when one considers a third dimension: regional politics. Whatever the global strategic motives of the key exporters, however important the North-to-South shift of economic power in enlarging the flow of arms, the impact at the regional level of arms transfers to the Third World will increasingly be the most important reason for control. The likelihood of regional conflicts among developing countries will undoubtedly remain high throughout the 1980s. Persistent tensions in the Middle East, Korea, Southern Africa, the Horn of Africa, Southeast Asia, and the Indian Subcontinent, plus potential disputes in the Persian Gulf, East Africa, the Maghreb, and South America, all indicate an increased likelihood that arms imported from the North will see use in the South in the coming years.

[5] The most notable example, of course, is the treatment of the oil producers by the West. The courtships of Algeria and Libya by the Europeans, and of Iran, Saudi Arabia, and Nigeria by the United States, are essentially efforts to extend to these developing countries an equity share in the international political economy which they will not want to jeopardize by manipulating the supply and price of oil.

9

It is often suggested that the use of arms transfers by the great powers to stabilize a given regional situation represents an alternative to directly involving the great powers or to allowing the situation to develop according to the indigenous strengths and weaknesses of the states of the region. Were the key arms exporters interested *only* in Third World regional stability and security—clearly they normally do have such an interest, but among many interests—one could be reasonably confident that the kinds, numbers, and destinations of arms to be shipped would be determined in a way that would strengthen the weak, deprive the strong, and generally favor defensive over offensive uses of forces. But this concept of arms-for-stability is not faithfully pursued in practice. The principal exporters of arms tend to have strong interests in dealing with the increasingly potent Third World states (Iran, Brazil, Nigeria, India, Saudi Arabia, Israel, Zaire, Indonesia) for several reasons: these are the states that are the prizes of Soviet-American geostrategic competition for influence in the Third World; they are the very Southern states whose economic ascendance nominates them for special relationships with industrialized states that respect, if not fear, their growing power; they can offer bureaucrats and arms industrialists attractively large and long-term transactions; and, irrespective of the size of individual deals, they can afford more and better arms because they have sufficiently large and experienced military establishments. Thus, Washington preaches regional stability but expands its arms commerce with Iran, Brazil, and others; Moscow continues to nourish Indian military strength long after the South Asian balance of power has shifted overwhelmingly in New Delhi's favor. The exporters vie for the contracts of dominant regional states, and the powerful in the Third World grow more so while regional stability becomes little more than a slogan of public justification and academic rumination.

The problem, then, is that while the causes for arms trade emerge from East-West political and North-South political-economic forces, the effects, largely harmful and destabilizing, are at the regional security level. The principal importers of arms—the Irans, Israels, and Brazils—have relatively little interest in the grand issues of East versus West and South versus

North. They are guided, variously, by their own national aspirations and concerns: to dominate regional politics, to survive and prosper in a hostile regional environment, to replace the great powers as the arbiters and guarantors of regional security in the Third World, and occasionally, to bully or batter weak neighbors. Thus, it is not the diffusion of power from North to South so much as the *uneven* diffusion of power throughout the South that makes arms trade a problem.

The Costs and Risks of Control

In determining the desirability and the design of measures to control international arms transfers, one must be sensitive to the fact that "solving the problem" might give rise to other problems. To some degree, the potential costs and risks of control can be reduced by judicious design and by patient efforts to nurture broad consensual support for restraint among a variety of international actors and interests. Still, it must be recognized that effective controls cannot be instituted without incurring at least some costs and running some risks, the severity of which must be measured against the expected benefits of control.

The most obvious risk in restricting international arms transfers is that of stimulating indigenous production of arms in the Third World, possibly creating more serious regional security problems than those that may stem from an active international arms trade. Few if any emerging Third World states with sizable perceived military needs could become self-sufficient in arms production in the 1980s, and in the area of the most advanced weaponry they will remain highly dependent on the advanced producers. But a growing number of Third World states will be acquiring the requisite skills to produce their own weapons, owing in part to the fact that as consumers in the international arms market, they are also recipients of heavy doses of military technology.[6]

[6]It is fair to say that a flourishing arms market increases the *capabilities* for indigenous production while a restrictive arms market would likely increase the *motivations* for indigenous production.

Indigenous production—primarily of simpler weapons (e.g., small arms, military vehicles, and munitions) but eventually of more advanced systems (anti-tank and anti-aircraft weapons, small naval craft, even tanks and aircraft)—will have considerable appeal to many of these states. Home production would reduce their vulnerability to political manipulation and future restrictive practices on the part of exporters, not to mention the risk of inadequate supply in the midst of a crisis. Additionally, investment in a domestic arms industry might be seen in Teheran, Brasília, New Delhi, and elsewhere as an investment in national power and prestige generally and, more specifically, in the sorts of productive processes, facilities, and technical and managerial skills that can contribute to economic-industrial development. Interest in domestic production is likely to be greatest in the very states that are now the key arms importers. And these are the states that are most capable of producing large quantities of fairly high-quality weapons, in part because of their relatively great national resources and in part because they have been the chief beneficiaries of the international diffusion of weapons technology. They are the Third World states which have client states of their own—clients who will themselves be purchasers of the products of these newly developing armaments industries. The unevenness of the spread of arms via the international market is, if anything, exceeded by the potential unevenness of the distribution of indigenous production capabilities. The effect of strict control on international arms trade, were it feasible, might be the further deterioration of regional power equilibriums due to disparities in Third World domestic productive capacities.

If measures to control arms transfers cannot be designed in a way that avoids this problem, they should at least be designed so that regional instabilities resulting from uneven indigenous production can be averted by transfers to weaker states. While the preservation or restoration of regional stability has not in practice been the key determinant of the major exporters' arms sales policies, the transfer of arms *can* serve these purposes. Highly restrictive controls on arms transfers, especially control measures that are not easily modified or waived, could all but eliminate the capacity of outsiders to ensure regional security short of more direct forms of involvement (some undesirable, others—such as diplomatic initiatives—desirable but of dubious utility).

Relatedly, it must be recognized that some types of arms, by their technical nature, are generally stabilizing, especially those that can be more effectively employed for defensive than for offensive purposes. Control that is predicated only on considerations of the volume and distribution of arms transferred, while ignoring the question of the likely stabilizing-versus-destabilizing effects of the various *kinds* of arms, could result in more aggression and violence among recipients than would no control at all.

Perhaps most disturbing is the danger that a more restrictive international market in conventional arms might prompt additional states to acquire nuclear weapons, an option that is becoming increasingly available to a growing number of states as the means to develop nuclear weapons are diffused along with the spread of civilian nuclear technology. The acquisition or suspected development of nuclear weapons by certain states (notably India, Israel, and South Africa) in conflict-torn regions has already aroused the concern of non-nuclear neighbors and is increasing the pressures on suppliers to export more and better weapons—to the neighbors in order to dissuade them from also acquiring nuclear weapons, as well as to the new or prospective nuclear states in order to reduce the risks that they will use their nuclear weapons in future combat for lack of adequate conventional military alternatives. As Cahn and Kruzel observe, the more likely it appears that certain states (Iran, Brazil, Pakistan, and South Korea, for example) will acquire nuclear weapons the more difficult—indeed, the less advisable—it may be for suppliers to restrict sales of conventional arms. However, paradoxically, the more and better conventional arms these prospective proliferants receive and the more their national power grows as a result, the less likely it is that they will be satisfied with non-nuclear status. In other words, conventional arms may whet rather than stifle the nuclear appetite, especially when so-called threshold weapons (those that are potentially useful for delivering nuclear explosives, such as bombers, attack aircraft, surface-to-surface

13

missiles) are made available. Still, the risks of stimulating nuclear proliferation must be carefully weighed in conceiving and implementing measures to control the conventional arms market.

To a significant extent, arms transfers provide a means for balancing international accounts between deficit countries in the North and surplus countries, particularly oil producers, in the South. In the absence of compensatory "recycle" mechanisms, the desire to control arms trade must be tempered by consideration of the account-clearing value of North-South sales. Moreover, as noted above, arms transfers also provide a means by which emerging and potentially disruptive Third World states, especially the major raw materials producers, can be induced to husband their power responsibly. Efforts by producers to control arms transfers should perhaps be coordinated with the promotion of alternative sorts of independent relationships (such as energy-related or agriculture-related technology transfer, or management assistance) that would not only benefit recipients but also give them a stake in international prosperity and tranquility.

Finally, "control without representation"—restrictions on arms trade devised by certain nations and imposed on others—could have severe adverse political ramifications as well as doubtful durability. Controls established by the superpowers alone, by all or most exporters, or by narrow coalitions of exporters and importers and not shaped by the interests of other states whose security is affected will be seen as—and may well be—arbitrary, discriminatory, and hegemonic. This will be particularly true of collaboration among exporters insofar as it results in market restrictions that are imposed on importers.

These caveats notwithstanding, it would be extremely difficult to argue that some control—indeed, considerable control—would be worse than none. Even if certain arms transfers do not upset regional security conditions, to sustain a level of security at a low level of armaments is plainly preferable—to all but arms merchants and generals—to sustaining the same level of security with larger quantities of arms. And there is ample reason to expect that higher arms levels more often than not reduce security, as military establishments grow in political power, as distrust between neighbors intensifies, and as regional powers in the Third World

14

accumulate more and better weapons than their smaller, poorer, already weaker neighbors. But control must be carefully designed and implemented, lest it prove counterproductive, ineffective, or too costly in terms of other values.

Dimensions of Control

The contributors to this volume offer a number of proposals for controlling arms trade, based on the shared premise that while many arms transfers may be desirable, an unrestrained pattern of arms transfers would ultimately disrupt international security as well as undermine efforts at economic development, nonproliferation, and control of terrorism. The difference in prescriptive emphasis between Dawkins and Huntzinger—the former on exporter restraint, the latter on regionally focused recipient restraint—stems in part from the fact that their 1980s Project assignments specified these particular emphases and in part from what seems to be a difference of opinion as to how and among whom effective control measures could be set in motion. Anne Cahn and Joseph Kruzel, whose essay is more predictive than prescriptive, offer a few proposals akin to those of Dawkins and Huntzinger but place greater emphasis on the possibilities for unilateral restraint by the world's principal arms exporter, the United States.

Peter Dawkins makes four proposals. His first is aimed at altering the economic motivation for arms exports. He argues that many arms producers, particularly the Western European states, export because their domestic requirements for weapons are too small to sustain the continuous, large-scale production necessary for their arms industries to be commercially viable. Dawkins therefore prescribes the implementation of a long-debated program of standardization and specialization in weapons production among NATO countries.[7] Such action would not in itself be

[7] With individual NATO countries specializing in the production of certain military goods to be used throughout the Alliance, while discontinuing production of weapons in which other NATO states—by mutual agreement—are specializing, large-scale national production bases could be sustained without having to rely on exports outside the North Atlantic market. Reduced competi-

15

enough to transform the present buyers' market into a sellers' market, since balance-of-payments motivations for arms transfers by the West to the Third World would persist and a reduced "need" to export may not reduce the desire for greater revenues. Moreover, a collective agreement among NATO producers, made possible by standardization, to curtail sales of advanced weapons systems could be undermined if the Soviets offered comparably sophisticated systems. Nonetheless, in the many areas of weapons technology where the Soviets do not compete and in those arms-importing regions where, for political or ideological reasons, the Soviets are not in the market, reduced competition among Western suppliers would increase their potential leverage in regulating arms traffic.

Dawkins' second proposal is for cooperation among suppliers to coordinate their arms-export policies on a region-by-region basis with the objective of maintaining regional stability.[8] (Again, NATO standardization and specialization might facilitate such collaboration.) Coordinated arms-export policies could discriminate in favor of weaker states; in highly conflictual regions, only defensive systems (to the extent that they can be distinguished from offensive systems) could be transferred; in regions where highly advanced technologies have not yet appeared, their export could be banned altogether unless it were clear that such technologies would enhance regional military equilibrium. Dawkins also recognizes the desirability of cooperative producer-recipient restraints in certain regions, and in this respect his proposal complements those of Jacques Huntzinger for regional recipient restraint.

Dawkins admits that regional producer restraints could be easily undermined if the Soviets did not subscribe. And he concedes that East-West political and ideological competition might preclude agreement on how to define "stability" in every

---

tion among suppliers would enable them to place tighter restrictions on weapons exports.

[8]Cahn and Kruzel prescribe a similar but unilateral policy of regional restraint for the United States involving the use of nonmilitary aid as a tool of enforcement, based on the belief that linking aid increases to cuts by recipients in their military expenditures would help slow regional arms races.

region and on how—or whether—it is to be maintained through arms transfer policies.[9] Still, he believes that Western and Eastern arms-exporting countries do have certain common interests that create possibilities for arms export restraint: the prevention of nuclear proliferation and regional nuclear war, and the prevention of terrorism. At a minimum, he argues, East-West agreement might be reached on banning sales of so-called nuclear threshold technologies—those weapons systems that could be used to deliver nuclear warheads—and on sales of miniature ("handheld") precision-guided munitions (such as surface-to-air missiles) to terrorist groups or to governments that might retransfer these weapons to such groups.

Dawkins' final proposal is for an agreement among arms producers to place more stringent controls on the retransfer of arms by recipients. Again, such a restriction might be better maintained if NATO standardization/specialization were implemented, for reduced competition among suppliers would increase their leverage over recipients, even in today's era of commercial transactions.

In Dawkins' view, his four proposals taken together constitute a modest, realistic framework for producer restraints on conventional arms trade in the 1980s. He argues that supply is more susceptible to regulation than demand, and that restricting supply, therefore, should be pursued despite its paternalistic implications. Cooperation among producers might not eliminate demand for arms—which is driven by regional security concerns and hegemonic aspirations—but it could help reduce demand somewhat (by promoting balanced regional arms levels) or at least deflect demand away from the more destabilizing and highly destructive weapons technologies.

Cahn and Kruzel believe that many of the same objectives could be fostered by American unilateral action, inasmuch as the United States is far and away the world's leading arms exporter. In addition to tying economic aid to reduced military spending and

[9] In fact, to put it more bluntly than Dawkins has, there is cause for doubt that Moscow would be averse to considerable regional *instability* in many areas, such as Latin America, Southeast Asia, and Southern Africa.

restricting retransfers of its arms exports, the United States should, in their view, set an example of self-abnegation for other arms producers by scrapping rather than exporting obsolete but potent weaponry. Cahn and Kruzel also propose the creation of a suppliers' code of conduct that would set guidelines limiting what technologies could be transferred and, perhaps, ceilings on aggregate exports as well, a measure that might be given institutional life by being coordinated with the NATO standardization/specialization process advocated by Dawkins.

Jacques Huntzinger's essay rejects the supply orientation of the other authors. He argues that the Third World's demand for arms in the 1980s will be too massive and too deeply rooted to be affected by producer restraint. In his view, efforts at control by suppliers will lead to expanded and possibly uneven domestic arms production in the less developed countries. Controlling arms transfers, then, must involve a reduction in the demand for arms if the ultimate goals—regional stability and reduced or averted militarization throughout the Third World—are to be achieved. Huntzinger offers three models of recipient restraint applicable to different types of regions, varying with respect to extant arms levels, the extent of reliance on internal initiative as opposed to external pressure, and the type of import restrictions—qualitative and quantitative—considered most politically feasible.

Under all of the Huntzinger models, outside arms producers would be expected to accede to the regional control agreement, lest they undermine the enterprise by promoting weapons sales that contravene the established regional restrictions. The models might be strengthened by inclusion of the suggestion of Cahn and Kruzel that producers take a more active role in respect of regional recipient restraint, namely, a commitment not to promote sales to the region, not to sell arms to renegade members of the regional group, not to sell arms to any member of the region without regionwide approval, and to apply the same quantitative and qualitative restrictions to arms transfers to nonsignatories. Producer action could also complement recipient restraint insofar as restrictions on exports of the most advanced and destabilizing weapons and of nuclear threshold systems could redirect consumer demand toward systems less dangerous for regional security. As well, export restraint would help to suppress demand in general insofar as Third World national security concerns were relieved by the reduced availability of weapons to those developing states most likely to cause regional trouble.

There are difficult problems in structuring control on a regional basis. A narrowly and rigidly defined regional approach—even one involving cooperation between producers and recipients—may abort or prove ineffective if only because the security concerns of some states in a given region are often affected, if not largely determined, by the military postures of states lying outside the region's periphery. For example, the breakdown of the recent effort by the Andean countries at regional arms-import restraint can be linked, in part, to the military buildup of nonparticipant Latin American states, most notably Brazil.[10] A similar effort at regional restraint in, say, the Indian Subcontinent would likely founder for the same reason unless accompanied by Iranian restraint.

In fact, isolating specific regions is to a large extent an arbitrary procedure. For instance, how is one to define the "Middle East"? Could arms transfers to Israel and the front-line Arab states (Egypt, Syria, Jordan) be restricted if Saudi Arabia and Libya, the potential arsenals for the Arab world, were not subject to effective restraints? But would Saudi Arabia agree to limitations on its arms imports without a commitment by its Persian Gulf rival, Iran, also to show restraint? While Saudi Arabia and Iran might be willing, in principle, to cooperate with an effort at controlling arms imports as part of a settlement of the Arab-Israeli conflict, their other security concerns—vis-à-vis each other, the Soviet Union, and internal threats—might militate against acceptance of limits on their own arms imports.

Structuring restraint on a regional basis may be difficult and have its limitations, but it could work in a given region if arms exporters and extraregional recipients undertook not to subvert

---

[10]In 1974, at the initiative of Peru, several Andean countries declared their collective intention to establish restrictions on their arms levels and military expenditures. This event (the Ayacucho Declaration) did not significantly weaken the demand for arms among the states involved, many of whom—including Peru—have actually increased their imports in the wake of the declaration.

the enterprise. A collaborative approach (joint producer-recipient efforts at establishing a framework for regulating future arms transfers), rather than a paternalistic approach by exporters, would seem to offer the best prospects for minimizing the chances of future regional arms races and regional conflicts and for contributing to a more constructive relationship between North and South.

In this regard, it should be noted that the one dimension of control that is not directly examined in the essays that follow is the global dimension. While the past few years offer ample evidence that globalist approaches to international problems are often inappropriate, the limitations and pitfalls of organizing the control of arms transfers among exporters alone or along strict regional lines suggest a need for considering a global approach as a possible framework for, if not alternative to, subglobal efforts. A possible first step might be the creation of a forum under United Nations auspices, akin to and perhaps connected with the permanent Conference of the Commitee on Disarmament (CCD) in Geneva, devoted to exchanging information and ideas on the arms market and its control, to promoting producer respect for regional recipient restraint, and to putting pressure on extraregional (i.e., peripheral) states to associate with regional efforts or at least to show moderation in demand.

Another multilateral approach to restraining arms transfers might be action by lending agencies such as the International Monetary Fund or World Bank to make their nonmilitary economic assistance to developing countries contingent on restraint by those countries in purchases of arms from abroad. With arms transfers being conducted more and more on a cash basis, the IMF and World Bank might have great leverage in restricting the ability of many Third World countries to buy weapons. Yet, aside from smacking of developed-country paternalism, such a policy would have no effect on the capacity of oil-rich developing countries—the biggest importers, by far—and their allies to buy arms and might consequently lead to arms imbalances in such unstable regions as the Middle East. Moreover, it is doubtful that the Soviet and East European arms suppliers would cooperate in what would very likely be seen as an effort by the Western, industrialized world to dictate to the poorest Third World countries how to spend their money.

A more substantive—though for the near term perhaps hopelessly ambitious—global approach might be the negotiation of a formal multilateral agreement regulating conventional arms transfers. In addition to his regional recipes for controlling arms transfers, Huntzinger mentions, albeit with limited optimism and enthusiasm, the possibility of a conventional arms replica of the Nuclear Non-Proliferation Treaty (NPT). A conventional NPT need not specify precisely and comprehensively what arms may be acquired by whom from whom and in what numbers. Rather, at least at the outset, it might prohibit international transactions in certain weapons that are generally, if not invariably, "destabilizing." Attack aircraft and long-range surface-to-surface missiles, to cite two examples, are essentially designed and most likely to be used for offensive tactical purposes. The fact that such systems may also be used defensively, or to deter aggression, suggests a need for flexibility in the operation of an international ban on trade in presumably destabilizing arms categories. Similarly, provisions for waiving transfer restrictions might also be required so that arms producers could deter or offset indigenous production of proscribed arms by noncompliant states through transfers of comparable or countervailing systems to these countries' disadvantaged neighbors. Accession and adherence to an international agreement of this sort could be promoted by a compensatory easing of terms for transfers of weapons (such as, perhaps, anti-aircraft and anti-tank systems) that are, on balance, defensive and, hence, stabilizing.[11]

The most serious problem with a global effort to control arms transfers is not that it would not discriminate sufficiently among states according to how justifiable their needs are, but rather that it *would* discriminate in a most profound way between those states that, by virtue of their industrialization, rely on their own production and those states—the developing states—that must

[11]This would be analogous to the way in which non-nuclear states are encouraged to accede to the nuclear Non-Proliferation Treaty (NPT) by its guarantees of free access to civilian nuclear technologies upon ratification of the treaty.

look to the international market. However commendable the objective of suppressing local conflict in the Third World, what justice is there in any arrangement that curbs the spread of arms but not their continued accumulation by those who have the resources and experience to manufacture them? Whatever one's personal view is on this question, the fact is it would be extremely difficult politically to negotiate global approaches to controlling the arms market without provoking the vast majority of states to insist that the industrialized states curb their own conventional weapons programs and limit their arsenals. Such a linkage, however fair, would make progress toward controlling international arms transfers highly unlikely.

Thus we do not underestimate the institutional, technical, and moral obstacles to instituting even a modest agreement that would deal only with a narrow sector of the arms trade.[12] At the same time, the achievement of even a limited and leaky international agreement constraining arms trade, perhaps linked loosely to restraints on the arsenals of the industrialized states, would have benefits beyond the immediate value of reducing traffic in certain weapons categories. It would represent a major achievement in bringing exporters and importers together to seek common interests in curbing both supply and demand. It could provide a setting for further international efforts to develop more comprehensive, more effective, and more restrictive rules and procedures. It could isolate for special scrutiny the transfer policies of those exporters and importers that refused to subscribe to the basic principles and initial stipulations of the accord. It might even create the moral pressure to force such nonsignatories to provide de facto compliance with the terms of the treaty. Finally, an international agreement to restrain trade in certain weapons systems would indicate that a global forum for dealing with the international arms market could produce more than sterile debate.

[12]Such as: How would the effects of arms restraint on regional stability be monitored? By whom? With what authority? What institutions with what powers would provide enforcement? Who would decide when and where to make waivers in the interest of preserving or restoring stable security conditions in the face of a surge in indigenous arms production?

* * * * * * * *

Generally speaking, any collaborative effort at arms transfer restraint—be it among importers of a given region, among exporters, or among both groups together—would favorably affect the security relationships among the participants (unless, of course, such an effort ended in acrimonious failure). The exchange of information, the candid articulation of concerns, the challenging of "worst-case assumptions," the personal and professional contact, the experience of making even rhetorical or limited substantive progress, and the shaping of embryonic institutional forums (that could one day mature into active security apparatus) would all help to produce a climate more conducive to the lowering of distrust and the maintenance of peace.

But even failing collaborative efforts, there is much that individual states or subregional groups of states can do to restrain arms transfers in the immediate future. Each individual arms-exporting state can structure its policy-making process so as to ensure that the ramifications of each arms sale—its impact on regional security, on nuclear proliferation, and on other foreign policy objectives—are understood before the deal goes through. Producers can include more stringent retransfer provisions in export contracts. Other ways can be found to cement bilateral relationships. Self-restraint can be imposed on the export of destabilizing weapons systems. Individual recipients, too, can impose self-restraint on their weapons imports, perhaps curtailing purchases of destabilizing offensive systems that only fan the flames of a regional arms race. Even in the absence of broader regionwide cooperation, an India and a Pakistan, a Peru and a Chile, or an Egypt and an Israel could agree bilaterally to restrict arms purchases as a means of stimulating matching restraint by other importers in the region.

There is much that should be done, and there is much that can be done. The essays that follow begin the task of examining the nature and scope of arms trade in the 1980s and conceiving various ways of affecting its evolution.

Arms Trade in the 1980s

Anne Hessing Cahn and Joseph J. Kruzel

ONE

Introduction

Only one statement can be made with absolute certainty concerning international arms trade in the years ahead: The trade will continue. From the time of the ancient Israelites, who were forbidden by the Philistines from making swords and were forced to acquire them elsewhere, to the time of modern-day Israelis, who have come to rely heavily on supplies of United States armaments, trade in military weapons has continued without significant interruption. Throughout history, military advisors and material have been exchanged between clans, tribes, city-states, and nations. To say that arms trade will continue in the years ahead is hardly a daring prediction, but the size and nature of the trade are subject to a number of critical uncertainties.

One important question is whether arms trade will continue to be a major focus of concern in international politics. Will senior government officials and informed publics give the problem more or less attention in the future than they do now? What political and strategic considerations will influence potential suppliers and recipients of conventional weapons? What new technologies will be developed in the years ahead? Will the new weapons be stabilizing or destabilizing? Will they be difficult or simple to produce? What economic considerations will shape arms trade in the 1980s?

NOTE: This essay was written before Anne Hessing Cahn joined the U.S. Arms Control and Disarmament Agency. The views expressed are those of the author and do not necessarily reflect the views of the United States government or any of its agencies or departments.

27

Our study addresses these and other questions. The answers we provide are often tentative, sometimes equivocal, and occasionally even contradictory. We are far more confident of our questions than of our answers. No doubt the predictions and propositions advanced in this analysis will generate a considerable debate. But our essay will have served its purpose if it encourages a discussion of these issues and of the need and opportunities for regulating arms trade in the 1980s.

We begin by examining a number of different perceptions of the arms trade issue. The debate over how arms trade ought to be perceived is critical. Any changes in world sentiment, any coalescence of international opinion around any one perspective, will have profound implications for the world's arms trade.

A number of political and strategic considerations have long served to justify international trade in armaments. For both supplier and recipient nations, arms trade has usually symbolized a cordial political relationship. Supplier states have derived, or at least have thought they derived, political influence from arms transfers. Another rationale for foreign military assistance has been the need to buy military rights in other countries.

These political and strategic rationales may undergo important changes during the 1980s. In addition, military alliances, while continuing to be an important element of international security, may have to alter doctrines and force postures in view of the future course of technology. The widespread incorporation of precision-guided munitions (PGMs) into weapons inventories may raise serious questions concerning the security of supply and the reliability of remote allies. Future world arms trade will depend critically on how supplier and recipient nations view their strategic requirements and how they perceive their political obligations.

Predictions about the future of conventional arms trade must also take account of the possible proliferation of nuclear weapons in the years ahead. The relationship between conventional arms trade and nuclear proliferation, particularly the possibility of using arms trade as a means of deterring the spread of nuclear weapons, is an idea worth exploring in some detail.

Our evaluation of arms trade in the 1980s includes a preview of the conventional weapons technologies that may become avail-

28

able for export during that decade and an analysis of whether they will be stabilizing or destabilizing. If future weapons improve defensive capabilities and stabilize a military balance, then the transfer of such weapons should be actively encouraged. On the other hand, if the new weapons increase the risk of war, international trade ought to be restricted as much as possible. We also need to know how complex future technologies will be. If there will be only a few nations capable of producing a weapon in the 1980s, some restriction of trade may be feasible. Alternatively, if many nations are capable of building a future weapon, any attempt at restraint might serve simply to stimulate indigenous production.

Our analysis will also consider possible changes in the economic dimensions of arms trade during the 1980s. If economic incentives for arms trade become more compelling, then political and moral restraints are likely to diminish. One crucial issue is, of course, the economic importance of arms trade to various producer nations: Will the industrialized nations be more or less dependent on arms trade as a means of acquiring hard currency? Will there be more or fewer suppliers of military weapons in the international market of the 1980s? Can other industrialized nations stay competitive with the United States and the Soviet Union in the production of sophisticated and expensive military equipment? What are the prospects for improved standardization among NATO arms producers? If standardization does progress, what will be the impact on future arms sales? Will developing nations be better able to satisfy their own weapons demands in the future? What sorts of collaborative production arrangements might such states work out with industrialized nations? Which states will have the biggest appetites for arms in the 1980s? Which will have the greatest capacity to pay? Our economic assessment concludes with a case-by-case analysis of nations whose arms acquisitions in the coming years may be particularly important to regional stability.

After each of these dimensions—perceptual, political, technical, and economic—has been analyzed, we assess the interactions between them and sketch out the most likely profile of conventional arms trade in the 1980s. Our concluding summary will describe the weapons that are likely to be traded and the producers, the consumers, and the "rules of the game" of arms trade. The essay ends with a look at possible opportunities for control of the arms trade and some recommendations for United States policy in the years ahead.

CHANGES IN ARMS TRADE SINCE WORLD WAR II

Arms trade in the mid-1970s differs significantly from the trade that occurred in the first two postwar decades. The *quantity* of trade is much larger now, and the relative *quality* of the weapons being exchanged is much improved. There are also significant differences in the method of paying for imported arms, in the amount of formal government involvement in the arms trade business, and in the types of states that are the major arms recipients.

The value of arms delivered worldwide has increased fourfold since 1961, from $2.4 billion to about $9 billion in 1975 (estimated in 1974 United States dollars).[1]

In 1970 total United States arms transactions amounted to about $4 billion (1970 United States dollars). In 1974 and again in 1975, the United States signed orders to sell or give away over $11 billion in military weapons and ancillary support. In 1975 the Soviet Union transferred over $5 billion of military equipment, France over $4 billion, and Great Britain about $1.5 billion (again, in 1970 United States dollars).

The qualitative aspects of the international arms trade have changed just as dramatically. In the 1950s and 1960s, supplier nations normally gave or sold obsolescent equipment to their clients, largely motivated by the desire of suppliers to clear their own inventories in order to absorb newer and more sophisticated armaments. In contrast, much of the recent arms trade consists of front-line new technology systems. Sales contracts are sometimes negotiated even before the prototypes are assembled.

[1] *The International Transfer of Conventional Arms,* a Report to the Congress, U.S. Arms Control and Disarmament Agency (ACDA), April 12, 1974, p. ix, and *World Military Expenditures and Arms Transfers, 1966–1975,* U.S. Arms Control and Disarmament Agency, Washington, D.C., p. 3. Their figures are based on deliveries and do not reflect the mid-1970 surge in orders.

Front-line technology has become the cutting edge of arms sales competition in the mid-1970s primarily as a consequence of the OPEC oil price increases in 1973 and 1974. The fourfold increase in the price of oil created more than a dozen newly rich nations with excess foreign currency reserves. For reasons of perceived security needs, prestige, and rapid development, many of these states sought to acquire up-to-date armed forces. Their willingness to pay cash for new weapons created a buyers' market in international arms trade. The oil-rich nations have been willing to purchase their weapons from nearly any willing supplier nation, thus making the arms marketplace exceedingly competitive.

The trend toward rapid diffusion of military technology accelerated during the 1970s. The United States did not release the tube-launched, optically tracked, wire-guided (TOW) anti-tank missile to Israel—perhaps its closest client in the arms trade business—until the last critical days of the 1973 Yom Kippur War. Eighteen months later, the missile had been approved for export to more than 20 nations. Another example is the sale of the F-14 fighter to Iran, the contract for which specified that technical improvements of the plane, avionics, and missile system would continue until the date of delivery. The United States is not alone in trading its latest military technologies. The Soviet Union exported the MiG-23, its most sophisticated tactical fighter aircraft, within two years of the plane's becoming operational.

These increases in quality and quantity of arms trade have rapidly spread sophisticated arms around the world. In 1964, only 9 developing nations had supersonic military aircraft in their inventories; by 1974, 41 developing countries possessed such aircraft or had them on order. Table 1 shows a similar proliferation of surface-to-surface missiles, from 8 countries in 1964 to 32 by 1974.

The improvement in military forces in recent years has been particularly dramatic in a few countries. Iran was perhaps the most spectacular case. Starting with a poorly equipped military establishment in the 1960s, by 1975 Iran had acquired 427 supersonic aircraft, 1,200 main battle tanks, more than 700 surface-to-surface missiles, and more than 700 helicopters. Comparable increases occurred in the increasingly isolated states of South

31

TABLE 1
Proliferation of Major Weapon Systems
in the Developing World
(year weapon first in inventory)

Country	Supersonic Aircraft*	Surface-to-Surface Missiles†
Israel	1955	1956
India	1958	1969
Taiwan	1958	1961
Cuba	1962	1961
Egypt	1962	1962
Pakistan	1962	1965
Iraq	1963	1972
South Africa	1963	—
Indonesia	1964	1961
Algeria	1965	1967
Iran	1965	1966
Korea, North	1965	1969
Korea, South	1965	1959
Philippines	1965	—
Afghanistan	1966	1962
Argentina	1966	1965
Ethiopia	1966	—
Morocco	1966	—
Saudi Arabia	1966	1964
Thailand	1966	1973
Vietnam, North	1966	1972
Jordan	1967	1974
Syria	1967	1966
Vietnam, South	1967	1972
Kuwait	1968	1962
Lebanon	1968	—
Libya	1968	1968
Peru	1968	1973

TABLE 1
Proliferation of Major Weapon Systems
in the Developing World
(year weapon first in inventory)

Country	Supersonic Aircraft*	Surface-to-Surface Missiles†
Nigeria‡	1969	—
Sudan	1970	—
Brazil	1972	1966
Colombia	1972	—
Abu Dhabi	1973	1974
Bangladesh	1973	—
Singapore	1973	1972
Uganda§	1973	1973
Venezuela	1973	1969
Somalia	1974	—
Ecuador	On order	—
Malaysia	On order	1971
Zaire	On order	—
Chile	—	1964
Tunisia	—	1970
Brunei	—	1972

*Supersonic aircraft include F-4 Phantom, F-5 Freedom Fighter, F-5E Tiger II, F-101 Voodoo, F-104 Starfighter, A-4 Skyhawk, Mystère IV A, Super Mystère, Vautour II, Mirage 5, Mirage F1, Jaguar, Lightning, Buccaneer, MiG-21, MiG-23, Su-7, and Su-9.

†Surface-to-surface missiles include anti-tank and naval surface-to-surface missiles: Aerospatiale (Nord) MM-38 Exocet and Entac, SS.10, SS.11, SS.12, Samlet, SS IC "Soud," Honest John, Hughes TOW, Contraves Sea Killer, Dassault MD-660, IAI Gabriel, Matra/OTO Melara Otomat, Shorter Seacar, SS-N-2 "Styx," At-1 "Snapper" and "Sagger," BAC Vigilant, MMB Bo 810 Cobra 2000.

‡There are only unconfirmed reports of Su-7s from the Soviet Union, via Egypt, to Nigeria in 1969.

§Uganda did not receive supersonic aircraft directly from a supplier nation, but rather received eight F-5 fighters from Libya as a gift in 1973.

SOURCE: *Arms Trade Registers: The Arms Trade with the Third World*, Stockholm International Peace Research Institute, 1975.

33

Africa and Taiwan; the Middle East combatant countries, including Libya; the South American nations of Argentina, Brazil, Peru; and the antagonistic NATO allies of the southern flank, Greece and Turkey.

Although more than 50 nations are currently active arms exporters, the Soviet Union and United States together account for 75 percent of the world's arms trade.[2] The addition of France and Great Britain raises this figure to 85 percent.

The 1970s have also witnessed a significant shift in the direction of arms transfers. United States arms transfers from 1945 to 1960 were primarily to Western European allies and nations on the perimeter of the Soviet Union. During the 1960s, only a third of United States arms exports went to NATO allies; another quarter was shipped to allies in Southeast Asia. Less than 10 percent went to the Middle East. In the same period, the Soviet Union concentrated its arms trade on Warsaw Pact allies (34 percent), Indochina (12 percent), and the Middle East (23 percent).[3]

Since 1972 the Middle Eastern and Persian Gulf countries have received by far the greatest share of arms exports. United States orders in fiscal year 1976 were approximately $9 billion, of which nearly 65 percent were from countries in the Middle East–Persian Gulf region. The Soviet Union also shifted its arms trade emphasis: by 1973 more than 80 percent of all major Soviet weapons exports to developing countries were delivered to the Middle East.[4]

This change in the direction of exports has had two important consequences. First, there has been a growing controversy over the very purposes of arms trade. In the earlier period, military aid given to America's closest allies enjoyed broad domestic support, owing to consensus on the importance to the United States of the survival of those nations. In the seventies, the bulk of United States arms transfers has gone to countries whose survival is not obviously vital to American security and foreign policy.

[2]Ruth Leger Sivard, *World Military and Social Expenditures, 1976,* W.M.S.E. Publications, Leesburg, Va., 1976, p. 5.

[3]*The International Transfer of Conventional Arms*, ACDA, p. 5.

[4]*Arms Trade Registers: The Arms Trade with the Third World*, Stockholm International Peace Research Institute (SIPRI), 1975, p. 155.

In the 1950s United States foreign policy goals with regard to Japan and the nations of Western Europe were straightforward and easy to articulate: to hasten their economic recovery, to assure their political stability, to enhance their abilities to resist communist aggression. These objectives were generally thought to be mutually reinforcing. In the 1970s American foreign policy goals in the Middle East and the Persian Gulf area are multiple, diverse, and often markedly conflicting. Washington wants to avoid a nuclear crisis with the Soviet Union and achieve overall stability, but also to lessen, counter, or forestall the influence of the Soviet Union; it wants to guarantee the survival of a strong Israel and also ensure the flow of oil to the United States and its allies.

The second difference is that in the fifties there was an apparent congruence between the primary foreign policy *goal*—rebuilding allies' capacities to defend themselves against communism—and the *means* for attaining those ends—providing the necessary arms. Today, because there are conflicting foreign policy objectives, the congruence between ends and means is often lacking. We simply do not know whether arms shipments to the Persian Gulf enhance regional stability or diminish it, whether arms furnished to Egypt reduce or enhance Israel's ability to survive.

There have also been changes in the method of paying for arms. During the 1950s most United States arms transfers were made in the form of outright grants. In the 1960s many of the previous aid recipients began to acquire military weapons and services by paying for them on credit. The oil price increases of the early 1970s enabled most OPEC nations to pay cash for their weapons purchases, and by 1975 cash sales accounted for 80 percent of total United States arms transactions. Outright grant aid steadily declined during the 1970s. In 1976 the U.S. Congress passed legislation that mandated the phasing out of all grant aid by the end of fiscal year 1977 unless subsequently authorized by Congress on a case-by-case basis.

One recent innovation is third-party financing of arms transactions. At the October 1974 Arab summit conference in Rabat, the oil-rich states—Saudi Arabia, Kuwait, Abu Dhabi, Qatar, and Libya—pledged $2.35 billion per year for four years to the front-line Arab countries—Egypt, Syria, and Jordan—and to the Palestinians. It is not clear whether these funds were actually disbursed, but the Arab OPEC states certainly have the capacity to finance major arms acquisitions by the confrontation states.

The Soviet Union also supplied much of its early assistance as grant aid. When Moscow supplied credit, it was generally extended for 10 to 12 years, at low (2 to 2½ percent) interest rates, repayable in hard currency, in commodities, or in local funds. In the 1970s the Soviet Union began to demand and receive hard-currency cash for its arms transactions.

The degree of governmental control of arms transactions has also changed. Before World War I, arms trade was generally the domain of private arms manufacturers. During the 1930s, in reaction to widespread perception that private munitions makers played a major role in bringing about World War I, national governments began monitoring and licensing the export of arms. By the mid-1970s, private arms sales accounted for less than 10 percent of the total, and most of the remaining private sales operated with at least implicit government approval.

In the United States, Congress is trying to reassert some influence over the formulation and implementation of arms transfer policies. During the 1950s and 1960s, Congress actively participated in the process, since funds for grant military assistance and for credit sales had to be appropriated by both the Senate and the House of Representatives. When the transition to cash transactions occurred in the 1970s, Congress lost most of its say in arms trade policies. But as United States arms sales rose rapidly, Congress sought to resume a more active role. In 1974 Congress approved an amendment to the Foreign Military Sales Act sponsored by Senator Gaylord Nelson. The Nelson Amendment requires the executive branch to notify Congress of any government-to-government arms sales valued at $25 million or more. Congress could, within 20 days of notification, veto the proposed sale by a concurrent resolution. Legislation passed by the 94th Congress in 1976 extended the Nelson Amendment provisions to cover all "major defense equipment" valued at over $7 million and lengthened the time available for congressional action to 30 calendar days.

These important recent changes in quality, quantity, direction, means of payment, and government involvement have dramatically altered the nature of arms trade. In the years ahead, equally striking and important changes may occur which could alter the magnitude of arms trade and its potential as an instrument of international stability or violence.

TWO

Changes in Perception

What makes arms trade a problem worthy of study at all? What is it about the transfer of military equipment across national borders that attracts public attention and concern?

Three reasons can be identified. First, there is a general assumption that higher armament levels increase the risk of war or at least increase the level of destruction should war occur. It is widely accepted, as an abstract principle, that the lower the arms level, the lower the likelihood of war. Thus there is widespread support for the notion that arms levels should be restricted however possible, including limits on transfers.

Second, arms transfers are often assumed to be more amenable to limitation than is indigenous arms production. Arms that cross national borders require agreement between two nations, supplier and recipient; the need for bilateral accord suggests an opportunity for restraint or limitation that does not exist when a nation builds and deploys its own new weapons.

Third, the fact that many developing nations buy arms abroad—even on favorable terms—seems like a woeful misallocation of scarce resources. The misuse of funds is all the more distasteful when someone seems to profit from the sale. Basil Zaharoff, archetypical merchant of death who made millions selling to both sides in the Boer War and World War I, is the standard image of the arms trader. This image is compounded by much of the popular literature on arms trade, which tends automatically to despair of increases in the volume of trade and the clandestine way in which many arms deals are consummated.[5]

The view of arms trade as a serious problem in its own right was reinforced in the early 1970s with the tremendous expansion in the international market. Arms producers seemed willing to make almost any deal with any nation. In their efforts to recapture petrodollars and improve balance-of-payments deficits, many arms-exporting nations seemed to turn a blind eye to concerns about the long-term consequences of their sales.

At the same time that popular concern about "arms for all nations" began to grow, a contrasting perspective also began to emerge. This point of view saw international arms trade not so much as a problem in itself but rather as a manifestation of other problems that recipient nations face. After all, many states do have legitimate reasons for wanting weapons. They may have disputed borders, face ideologically hostile neighbors, or confront domestic insurgencies. And even if developing nations do sometimes purchase military equipment exceeding their legitimate military needs, the developed countries have for a much longer time shown remarkably little restraint in their own appetites for weapons.

Those who see arms trade as a problem in itself tend to look to the arms-producer states for solutions. They feel that arms importers, particularly developing nations, cannot be trusted to define their own legitimate security interests or to make their own decisions concerning budgetary allocations. As Colin Gray has noted, many liberals feel that selling arms abroad is the modern-day equivalent of selling firearms and firewater to the Indians. This perspective implies that technically superior nations are more farsighted and more responsible; hence they are better able to make decisions about the weapons needs of the Third World than the developing nations are themselves.

The view that arms trade is not a proper focus of international concern is part of a world view that has gained considerable

---

[5] A good example is the *Time* cover story of March 3, 1975, "Guns for All: The World Arms Trade."

acceptance during the 1970s. The demands of developing nations for a new international economic order reflect a growing resentment toward the affluent industrialized nations of the world. Developing nations are demanding to be taken seriously. They will surely resist any future policy that seems to be motivated by paternalism on the part of more affluent nations. They are likely to resent any suggestion to restrain or regulate trade in armaments. Governments of developing nations expect their perceived security requirements to be considered legitimate.

In the United States the official attitude toward arms trade also changed dramatically between the mid-1960s and the mid-1970s. In the 1960s the general presumption within the United States government was against arms transfers. Advocates of a particular arms transfer were forced to make a persuasive case to critics before the sale or grant would be approved. By the mid-1970s the presumption had shifted. Voices of caution and restraint were on the defensive: in a general environment of permissiveness toward arms exports, the critics were obliged to argue vigorously against transfers. The bureaucratic interests in the United States government favoring arms restraint and economic development—the Arms Control and Disarmament Agency, the Agency for International Development—proved virtually powerless compared with the array of organizations—the Departments of State, Defense, Treasury, and Commerce—pressing other interests.[6] With the Carter administration, the arms trade pendulum started to swing back. Early arms sales decisions by the administration reversed a prior obligation to sell "concussion bombs" to Israel and denied Israel the right to export to Ecuador supersonic Israeli fighter planes with American engines.

When arms were mostly given as grant aid or sold on credit, a natural adversary relationship existed within the executive branch. Ceilings were fixed on the absolute levels of both military assistance and credit sales. More aid for one country generally

[6]Amelia Leiss, *Testimony: Foreign Assistance Authorization: Arms Sales Issues, Hearings before the Subcommittee on Foreign Assistance of the Senate Committee on Foreign Relations*, 94th Cong., 1st Sess., 1975, pp. 549–553.

meant less aid for another. Arms aid or credit sales to India, for example, may have been challenged by the Pakistan desk at the State Department. But with the shift to cash sales, this built-in bargaining process no longer operated.

Other nations that have been more reluctant suppliers than the United States might become more vigorous arms salesmen in the 1980s. West Germany, sensitive about its history of militarism, has long held to a policy of refusing to sell military goods in "areas of tension." But West German restraint has never prevented an interested buyer from acquiring arms; it has only led potential recipients to look elsewhere to satisfy their demands. When Germany rejected an Iranian request to buy Leopard tanks in 1974, Iran took its business to London and bought 800 British Chieftains. No one knows how long Bonn will continue to adhere to a policy of restraint that benefits its competitors economically and itself only by enhancing its self-image. The 1975 German agreement to build nuclear facilities in Brazil suggests that Germany is now willing to risk the displeasure of its major allies, especially the United States, by agreeing to transfer potentially dangerous items. Other arms producers with restrictive sales policies—Japan, for example—might also become more willing participants in the arms market in the 1980s, particularly if they find themselves confronted with chronic balance-of-payments difficulties.

Of course, some arms exporters might become more restrictive in the future. In France, the Catholic Church mounted a campaign against the government's willingness to sell conventional arms virtually without restrictions. Public opinion, activated by the church, could eventually cause a tighter government policy.

Policy making in supplier states would be greatly simplified if a proposed arms transfer could be judged either good (that is, stabilizing), bad (likely to increase the risk of war), or merely worthless (a squandering of natural resources with no effect on regional balance of power). But no arms transfer fits neatly into one category. There will always be disagreements over the character of weapons systems, and there will always be disputes over the definitions of "good," "bad," and "worthless." One nation's perception of stability may be another's definition of insecurity. One country's worthless weapons could be another's serious threat.

The assessment of a particular arms transaction ultimately depends on how the recipient government intends to employ the weapons. A regime could use arms to ensure its territorial defense, to compete in a local arms race, to aid in national development, to quell internal rebellion, to satisfy avaricious generals and admirals, to attack a neighbor, to become a regional great power. How the weapons are used depends on intentions of the recipient which may be difficult to discern and in any case may change very quickly. The new weapons may themselves serve to alter intentions. Improved military capabilities have often generated new foreign policy objectives.

Arms-exporting nations probably have no choice but to decide arms transfers on an ad hoc basis, to weigh the consequences of a proposed transfer to various parties, in both the long run and the short. Within this case-by-case approach, however, two marginal changes in attitudes may affect arms exports in the decade ahead. First, arms transfers whose impact is ambiguous or difficult to gauge are more likely to be approved in the future than they were in the past. As noted earlier, the burden of argument in the future will rest chiefly on those who oppose an arms sale. A stronger consensus on the likelihood of adverse consequences will be required to prevent an arms transfer in the 1980s.

Second, exporters will be less likely in the future to deny an arms transfer on the grounds that it is simply a waste of valuable resources. If a state wants to spend its money on guns, few suppliers will insist that the regime spend it on butter. For years the United States refused to sell supersonic combat aircraft to Latin America because there appeared to be no requirement for such high-performance weapons and because all available planes were needed in Vietnam. The policy was unsuccessful—Latin American countries acquired jets from other exporters—and caused considerable resentment toward the United States. To many North Americans the policy was laudable; to many Latin Americans it was demeaning and paternalistic, as though Uncle

Sam were reserving the right of supersonic flight to pilots of industrialized nations. Such restrictions, however well-intentioned, are less likely to be attempted in the near future.

The two contrasting perspectives of arms trade described in this section represent the poles of the contemporary debate. Few people, and even fewer governments, would subscribe completely to one point of view or the other. Most observers who see arms trade as a legitimate focus of attention would concede that many demands of arms importers are not excessive. And many of the developing nations that criticize restrictions on their arms imports are quick to demand that such restrictions be imposed on sales to their neighbors.

The debate about arms trade will undoubtedly continue through the 1980s. It is an important debate to follow. The pace and magnitude of arms trade in the years ahead will be determined at least as much by perceptual questions of whether trade is good or bad, moral or immoral, as it will by analyses of the strategic, technological, and economic considerations for and against control.

THREE

Strategic and
Political Considerations

Trade in armaments has traditionally symbolized a cordial political relationship, giving substance to treaty commitments or other intangible bonds of friendship. To some extent this is still true. Both the exporter and the importer expect to benefit from an arms deal. The recipient gets the weapons; the supplier state invariably hopes to derive some type of political influence resulting from gratitude on the part of the recipient or from a more tangible need. If the transfer requires a subsequent flow of spare parts or training of indigenous personnel, the recipient state may feel obligated to maintain good relations with the producer. Even if an arms transfer does not bring obvious benefits in terms of political influence, it may serve a preemptive function by denying influence to other, possibly less benevolent, supplier states.

The influence derived from arms trade is not a constant and measurable asset, however. Political influence seems to be greatest when it is least needed. In a crisis the supplier nation may find itself with no special influence at all, as the United States learned during the 1974 Turkish invasion of Cyprus. Moreover, insofar as political influence does derive from arms transfers, it may turn out to be a liability rather than an advantage, as the United States painfully learned from its experience in Vietnam. While arms suppliers sometimes do wield significant influence over their clients, generally such influence is more a result of the diplomatic isolation of the arms recipient than of the arms transfer itself. United States influence over Israeli foreign policy is a good example.

‍ A supplier nation may also justify arms transfers on the military ground that additional weapons may make the recipient better able to defend itself and less likely to call upon the producer country to intervene militarily in a crunch. This was the basic rationale behind United States "grant aid," the major portion of United States arms transfers until the late 1960s. Arms transfers have an additional military benefit. If local defense were to break down and outside military help were required, it would be far better to have allied forces properly trained and equipped with compatible equipment.

Another rationale frequently advanced for foreign military assistance is the need to secure military "rights" in other countries. American aid to Pakistan in the 1950s was a quid pro quo for authority to base U-2 reconnaissance aircraft in the country. In 1975 the United States negotiated a five-year extension of base rights in Spain; it was no coincidence that the agreement was accompanied by an American offer to supply Spain with F-16s and other military equipment.

But there are at least two possible military objections to arms transfers from the supplier's point of view. First, massive transfers of arms to other countries can reduce the supplier's own military readiness. American military officials raised this concern when the United States undertook a massive and rapid resupply of Israeli military forces after the 1973 Yom Kippur War. American stockpiles and reserve inventories were so depleted that they will not be fully replenished until 1981. The resupply of Israel was an unusual occurrence, but if future wars consume military equipment at an even faster pace than they have in the past, resupply of dependent allies may compromise the preparedness of military forces in the supplier nation.

A second, less significant concern is limited to a few producer nations. Many arms transfers involve training of local military forces; indeed, most American arms deals entail greater expenditures on "infrastructure" items than on actual combat equipment. This training component of arms transfers requires a substantial number of military personnel from the supplier state. The

United States, which places much greater emphasis on training than does the Soviet Union, had many of its military personnel involved in such activities in the mid-1970s. As the size of the American military establishment declines and as military pay continues to increase, the cost of diverting such personnel will be increasingly questioned over the next few years. The United States has taken steps to phase out military advisory groups and to shift responsibility for training to civilian contractors. Other supplier states may follow suit.

Will the politico-military rationale for arms transfers change over the next decade? Certainly the influence-gaining rationale and its preemptive corollary—if we don't sell, others will—will remain important. So long as the oil-producing states of the Middle East continue to have revenues they want to spend on armaments, many suppliers will be happy to compete for whatever influence or goodwill—not to mention money—that attends such sales. Suppliers will also be interested in other, less wealthy nations in the world, particularly those with strategically important locations, such as the Philippines.

The rationale for securing foreign bases will undergo an interesting transformation in the years ahead. The number of bases that the United States maintains in foreign countries will almost certainly continue to decline over the next decade. Accordingly, there will be less need to use arms transfers as payment for such bases. At the same time, the reduced military presence of the United States around the world may lead to the increased use of arms transfers as a means of projecting influence abroad. The United States will continue to be a global power in the 1980s, but its strength will depend less on pure military power and the threat of intervention and more on economic and diplomatic leadership. Increased arms transfers may be a means of compensating for a global military retrenchment. The Soviet Union faces a different situation. If Moscow continues to expand its global interests, it may find a need for more foreign military bases and thus for increased arms exports and other assistance to host nations.

Predictions about the future of conventional arms trade must take account of another possible development of the 1980s: the proliferation of nuclear weapons. Could the transfer of conventional arms be used to impede the further spread of nuclear weapons? It seems doubtful that threats to cut off the flow of conventional arms would deter many nations from crossing the nuclear threshold. In fact, such a threat might actually stimulate nuclear proliferation in that a non-nuclear state unable to satisfy its demand for conventional arms might turn to nuclear weapons in frustration.

This quandary suggests the discouraging proposition that the only means of retarding nuclear proliferation may be to encourage conventional proliferation, to make arms trade as unfettered as possible. But even that policy might backfire. The unlimited transfer of conventional arms could conceivably stimulate nuclear proliferation by whetting a nation's appetite for weapons of all types. It is also possible that large-scale transfers of conventional arms to one nation might stimulate a neighboring state to consider nuclear status as a "quick fix" for inferiority in conventional weapons.

One compromise strategy is conceivable. Arms-producing nations might consider linking the issue of conventional arms transfers to adherence to the Nuclear Non-Proliferation Treaty (NPT). Producers of conventional arms would sell their wares only to nations that had ratified the NPT. Article IV of the treaty gives the non-nuclear signatories preferential treatment in securing the benefits of peaceful uses of nuclear energy; giving such states preferential treatment on conventional arms transfers would be a consistent and complementary undertaking.

There are a number of drawbacks to such a scheme. In its absolute form the proposal would preclude arms transfers to all nonsignatories of the NPT. This would prohibit United States arms transfers to Israel and Soviet transfers to Egypt, a restriction that both suppliers might find unacceptable. Another difficulty is that the proposal would not affect arms transfers by France and China, since neither has signed the treaty. Without the accession of Paris and Peking, such a plan might offer those nations a convenient opportunity to expand their arms markets. The proposal would also stimulate the indigenous production of weapons by nonsignatories of the NPT such as Brazil and India and accelerate their development as major arms exporters. Fi-

48

nally, if the major producers were to prohibit the transfer of conventional arms to nations genuinely concerned about their security, the effect might be to drive such nations to develop nuclear weapons and rely on them more heavily than they might otherwise have done.

The impracticability of such a nontransfer proposal demonstrates an important paradox about conventional arms trade and nuclear proliferation. If more countries acquire nuclear weapons in the 1980s, as now seems probable, it may well be more prudent, in the interest of global stability, for the major producers of conventional arms to become less rather than more restrictive in their trading policies. Freer trade in armaments would encourage greater levels of conventional arms, but it might also reduce the chance of a nuclear weapon being detonated in anger. It is a sad but unavoidable reflection of future trends that the ability of arms-producing nations to restrict arms trade is likely to diminish as nuclear capabilities spread.

FOUR

Technology

Throughout history, weapons technology has generally advanced at a slow and measured pace. There have been long intervals when little or no improvement occurred in the design of weapons. For example, the typical naval warship of the mid-nineteenth century—a wooden sailing vessel with a smooth-bore cannon—was in most respects strikingly similar to warships built a century earlier.

When advances in military technology occur, they are usually minor improvements of existing weapons rather than dramatic breaks with the past. In the first 25 years after World War II, most advances in conventional armaments were simply improvements of technologies developed during the war. Weapons and delivery systems grew bigger, more complex, and much more expensive, but without undergoing any quantum improvement in military effectiveness.

A new class of conventional weapons is currently being introduced that seems to constitute a major break with the past. The weapons are called *precision-guided munitions* (PGMs)—in effect, weapons that are terminally guided to their targets—and they offer a significantly higher probability of kill than earlier munitions. In 1974 Dr. Malcolm Currie, the Pentagon's director of research and development, claimed that PGMs had brought weapons technology to the threshold of a "true revolution in conventional warfare."[7]

[7]Quoted in Phil Stanford, "The Automated Battlefield," *New York Times Magazine*, February 23, 1975, p. 12.

51

To understand the future of conventional arms trade, it is necessary to understand PGMs and other new conventional technologies and the extent to which they actually do portend a revolution in warfare. It is also important to know what impact the weapons of the future will have on military stability and whether such weapons will be more or less expensive than the weapons currently in military arsenals.

PRECISION–GUIDED MUNITIONS

The first PGMs to attract public attention were the "smart bombs" used by the United States in the late stages of the Vietnam War. PGMs—in particular, anti-tank and anti-aircraft weapons—also figured in the Yom Kippur War of 1973. On the basis of these two experiences, many defense experts quickly predicted that PGMs would be the decisive weapon of the future. Within a few years, however, these same specialists had begun to reassess the role of PGMs. Some now argue that PGMs were overrated. They say that the new weapons might reinforce existing trends in conventional warfare but would not force drastic alterations.[8]

At this writing, there remains substantial disagreement over the general impact of PGMs on military strategy. No one knows whether they will increase or reduce the risk of war in the 1980s and whether they will heighten or depress the level of damage if a war breaks out. Five propositions that are frequently advanced about PGMs have particular relevance to arms trade and are worth considering in some detail.

Proposition 1: PGMs favor the defense over the offense If this proposition is true, several important consequences follow. Regional hostilities may lead to war less often if militarily inferior nations are better able to defend themselves against superior forces. "Crisis stability" may be enhanced; there will be reduced

[8]James F. Digby, *Precision-Guided Weapons*, Adelphi Paper 118, International Institute for Strategic Studies, London, 1975, pp. 3–4. See also James L. Foster, *The Future of Conventional Arms Control*, Rand Paper p-4389, The Rand Corp., Santa Monica, Calif., August 1975.

incentives for preemptive attack. If PGMs do favor the defense, their transfer should be encouraged since such weapons would provide defense dominance at low cost. Unfortunately, this proposition is subject to several important qualifications.

First, the very terms "offense" and "defense" are ambiguous. Strategic defense in some cases may be very different from tactical defense. An attacking nation may be in a defensive posture over most of the battlefront; a defender may occasionally be forced into offensive tactical maneuvers. As Egypt demonstrated in the Yom Kippur War, anti-aircraft and anti-tank weapons can be used offensively as well as defensively. Second, the value of PGMs depends heavily on the tactics, structure, and other armaments of both sides engaged in a conflict. It has been argued that given the existing balance of forces between NATO and the Warsaw Pact, the introduction of PGMs by both sides would actually work to the relative benefit of the Warsaw Pact.[9] Finally, while current PGMs may on balance appear to favor the defense, it is less certain that future PGM generations will do so.

Proposition 2: PGMs will make the use of high-performance, high-cost armaments prohibitively expensive There is a compelling superficial logic to this proposition. A $10 million aircraft that can easily be destroyed by a $10,000 PGM will certainly not be a cost-effective investment. If PGMs live up to the expectations of their most enthusiastic proponents, the international demand for high-performance, high-cost aircraft and tanks should decline considerably over the coming decade. But this proposition, too, is subject to important qualifications.

In Europe, adverse weather conditions will make current PGMs effective less than half the time during daylight hours and virtually useless at night.[10] Also, as PGMs become more sophis-

[9]Steven L. Canby, *The Alliance and Europe: Military Doctrine and Technology*, Adelphi Paper 109, International Institute for Strategic Studies, London, Winter 1974/75, and "Regaining a Conventional Military Balance in Europe," *Military Review*, vol. 55, no. 6, June 1975.

[10]Steven L. Canby, *Terminal Guidance on the Battlefield: Obtaining Its Potential Payoff*, Technology Service Corp., Santa Monica, Calif., May 2, 1975, p. 1.

ticated, their price will rise drastically, making future cost-exchange ratios less lopsided. On balance, however, even a slight increase in the attrition rate of expensive weapons systems might make them an inefficient way to spend limited defense resources. PGMs may limit the appeal of sophisticated systems that can be used only in circumstances in which low rates of attrition are assured.

Proposition 3: PGMs will accelerate the pace of war-fighting; consumption of munitions may be many times greater than in non-PGM engagements This was one of the most widely touted lessons of the Yom Kippur War. But again, the popular image concealed important qualifications.[11] Most of the equipment losses in the Yom Kippur War were actually the result of non-PGM weapons. In addition, the battle tactics employed by both sides—repeated attempts at breakthroughs—unavoidably caused high losses of soldiers and material. The accelerated pace of combat was not especially related to the use of PGMs. Finally, the major losses in the 1973 war occurred in brief but intense battles; such engagements almost invariably create high losses regardless of the type of armament employed.

No one really knows yet what long-term effect PGMs will have on the consumption of munitions. There is a general suspicion, confirmed by the Yom Kippur War, that PGMs will increase the rate at which personnel and military hardware are consumed. This concern raises important questions about the future viability of military alliances. If PGMs do lead to a higher rate of consumption of military equipment, local allies may be forced to alter their defense posture. They will have to depend on either greater pre-positioning of replacement stock and spare parts or a secure and "warm" production line for such equipment. Greater pre-positioning may seem preferable in theory, but in practice it poses a serious problem. In addition to greater cost, large, fixed storage areas will be extremely vulnerable to attack by the enemy's own PGMs. Thus a nation that tries to improve its readiness by pre-positioning will thereby simultaneously make its arsenal a more tempting target for preemptive attack. The alternative to

[11]Steven L. Canby, private memorandum on James F. Digby's *"Precision-Guided Weapons,"* May 5, 1975, p. 7.

54

this "readiness-vulnerability" syndrome would be to rely on an ally removed from the potential area of conflict. In the case of Western Europe, this would mean greater dependence on the United States.

Increased reliance on a remote ally poses obvious political problems. It also raises serious military problems. In the 1980s will a remote ally be able to guarantee security of supply? If an opponent possesses long-range anti-aircraft and surface-to-surface PGMs, it may well be able to interdict air- or sea-borne resupply efforts either during transit or at the destination. The United States can no longer be assured a "free ride" to Western Europe in the event of hostilities.

It is difficult to gauge the net impact of the security-of-supply issue on the future of arms trade or on the future of alliances. A number of countries can produce PGMs, but the risk of storing large numbers of PGMs in the region of likely conflict may enhance the need for alliance with a relatively invulnerable supplier. At the same time, resupply may be a much more difficult problem if an adversary has PGMs. These uncertainties are not likely to be resolved in the near future, and so long as uncertainties persist, PGMs will probably serve more to strengthen than to weaken existing military alliances.

Proposition 4: PGMs will reduce collateral damage to population and industry If this proposition is true, it would constitute a significant reversal of the increasingly destructive trend of military technology and could be a reason to encourage rather than impede the international transfer of PGMs.

PGMs certainly present the capacity to limit collateral damage if a defender takes no appropriate countermeasures. On the other hand, against a defense employing more dispersion, more mobility, and more camouflage, an attacker might feel impelled to make greater use of "area weapons" with high collateral damage. There is also the problem of "sublimation": as forward-area targets become more difficult to locate and strike, attacks on rear-area targets could become more tempting.

There is also a broader question raised by the possibility of reduced collateral damage: Is such a reduction a desirable objective? Less collateral damage may serve to make war less devastating—hence a less appalling prospect. If the United States had possessed PGMs in 1962, for example, President Kennedy could have chosen a "surgical strike" against Soviet missile bases in Cuba rather than a blockade. PGMs may give national leaders a set of military options that will incline them more toward military action than toward diplomacy in a future crisis.

Proposition 5: PGMs will require sophisticated data processing capacities beyond the reach of most developing countries There has been a good deal of debate over the proper environment for the use of PGMs. Will the new weapons require an automated battlefield with sophisticated command and control systems, or will they best be employed by small mobile squads acting independently? The answer will obviously depend on the terrain and on other types of military forces and equipment available. PGMs will not have the same effect on the NATO–Warsaw Pact balance that they will have in the Middle East. However, one point is clear: PGMs are far less complex and much easier to operate than many high-performance systems now being transferred. Any military force capable of operating the American F-4 fighter can use many types of PGMs, and many countries that could not manage high-technology forces will find some kinds of PGMs within their technological ken.

None of these five propositions is unconditionally true, and on many points there remains a great deal of uncertainty and debate. The only definite fact is that the 1980s will be years of transition in conventional defense. Relatively simple PGMs will be widely available to military establishments around the world, and advanced PGMs will be developed which will probably overcome some of the more vexing technical problems of the 1970s. Terrain-matching terminal guidance may permit PGMs to operate at night and in adverse weather conditions, and remotely piloted vehicles employing television pictures may be used to attack moving targets.[12]

The 1980s will also be a time of doctrinal dispute for many military forces. Virtually every nation will debate whether PGMs should be introduced. Where the new weapons are introduced,

[12]Digby, *"Precision-Guided Weapons,"* pp. 3–4.

there will be disputes over how they should be integrated into existing force structures. PGMs may require reorganization of military forces—always a quarrelsome issue—and they will certainly spur budgetary debates between groups favoring PGMs and those preferring more traditional types of armaments. The U.S. Air Force stubbornly refused the introduction of PGMs into its weapons inventory for several years before using smart bombs, with notable success, in Vietnam.[13]

It is often asserted that rapid changes in military forces are the most destabilizing factors in local military confrontations. Some experts have suggested that the potential for miscalculation is increased more by the *rate* of change than the *amount* of change.[14] If that is true, then a rapid transition to PGMs would be an automatic prescription for disaster in many regional conflicts around the world. Fortunately, there are a number of factors that could slow the transition to PGMs and damp the attendant instabilities. The first is the cost of such systems. A single PGM—a TOW missile, for example—may be quite inexpensive as far as weapon systems go. But the cost of the launcher and supporting guidance equipment invariably multiplies the expense of the missile itself. The cost of equipping a military force with PGMs could be a substantial drain on the meager resources of many developing countries. As well, in many countries, bureaucratic and doctrinal reluctance will slow the introduction of PGMs. And finally, there are sufficient uncertainties about the impact of PGMs on battlefield strategy so that even states that have compelling theoretical reasons for acquiring PGMs may in practice exercise considerable caution in making the transition.

On balance, PGMs appear to be a relatively stabilizing development in military technology. The new systems will be more appealing to states that feel threatened by tactical air and armor capabilities and somewhat less appealing to nations with offensive intentions. There are fairly simple and relatively inexpensive PGMs that can help redress military inferiority, particularly in tactical air strength.

[13]See Graham T. Allison and Frederic A. Morris, *Precision-Guidance for NATO: Another Weapons Revolution?* draft paper.

[14]Leiss, *Testimony*, pp. 549–553.

But many of the virtues of PGMs—ease of operation, mobility, high probability of kill—may under some circumstances become perilous vices. Some PGMs are ideally suited for use by guerrilla or terrorist groups. In 1974 a group of Palestinian terrorists was discovered near the Rome airport with an SA-7 anti-aircraft missile. One possible safeguard might be to equip PGMs with Permissive Action Links (in essence, locks on individual weapons that require positive action to open before the weapon can be used) similar to those on United States tactical nuclear weapons deployed abroad; but the danger of unauthorized use would remain. Many nations confront internal threats of subversion or rebellion that are far more serious than any external threat they may face. States in this circumstance may well shun the acquisition of PGMs out of fear that the new weapons might fall into the wrong hands.

OTHER DEVELOPMENTS

A number of other conventional arms technologies will affect the nature of the arms trade in the 1980s. One is the cruise missile, a born-again World War II delivery system. The first cruise missile was the German V-1 "buzz bomb" used against British cities in the late stages of World War II. In the 1970s the cruise missile has attracted renewed attention for two reasons. First, a number of technical advances in the 1960s made cruise missiles far more efficient than they had been previously. Ironically, the second reason for renewed interest in cruise missiles was a reaction to arms control endeavors. Cruise missiles were not limited by the initial Strategic Arms Limitation Talks (SALT) accords. The available technology and omission from SALT-imposed limitations sparked American interest in the new weapon. By the mid-1970s advanced cruise missiles were under development only in the United States, but many other nations were capable of producing them, and many more—their interest stimulated by the United States program—will be able to do so by the 1980s.

The appeal of the cruise missile lies in its combined virtues of low cost and substantial versatility. The United States strategic cruise missile will probably cost about $1 million per copy; less sophisticated systems could be produced for even less. Cruise missiles can be used as strategic weapons or, when equipped with precision guidance, as tactical weapons. They can be armed with either conventional or nuclear warheads.

This versatility blurs the traditional distinctions between different types of warfighting and the weapons employed in each type of conflict. A missile that can be either strategic or tactical, conventional or nuclear, raises serious questions about the future viability of arms control agreements.[15]

The cruise missile also raises a number of questions concerning arms transfers. Do cruise missiles per se offer any new military options? Probably not. The cruise missile is little more than an inexpensive unmanned aircraft: it cannot perform missions qualitatively different from those performed by combat aircraft.

Should producer nations transfer versatile weapons systems that could be used in a strategic nuclear role? The development of precision guidance will make conventionally armed cruise missiles much more useful against a wide range of targets. But transfers of such systems will give recipients a useful means of delivering nuclear weapons if they should ever develop them. There is precedent for refusing to transfer such dual-capable systems. The U.S. Congress refused to authorize the release of Pershing missiles to Israel because such missiles could easily be fitted with nuclear warheads produced by the Israelis.

The third question concerns the prospects for limiting the transfer of cruise missiles. Producer nations in the 1980s will almost certainly be reluctant to export cruise missiles with a range greater than 1,000 miles. But the effectiveness of a limit on the transfer of short-range missiles is doubtful. The United States has about a 10-year lead in new cruise missile technology, but simple buzz bomb variety cruise missiles can be produced indigenously by a number of countries and little opportunity for effective limits on transfers seems possible.

Among the other conventional technologies that will become important in the 1980s are "area" weapons. Unlike PGMs, they

[15]For a useful analysis, see Richard Burt, "The Cruise Missile and Arms Control," *Survival*, vol. 18, no. 1, January–February 1976, p. 10.

are intended for use against dispersed targets. Perhaps the most dramatic new area weapon is the fuel-air explosive, or "concussion bomb" capable of creating blast overpressures of 300 pounds per square inch. Fuel-air explosives are an effective means of clearing helicopter landing sites and attacking hardened anti-aircraft positions.

Other new area munitions include cluster-bomb anti-personnel weapons (which could be used against large concentrations of troops) and air-scatterable mines (which could disable tanks and armored vehicles). Like PGMs, these new area weapons are relatively simple to design, produce, and use. There may well be a substantial demand for such weapons in the 1980s, and their transfer may be difficult to restrict.

In the early 1970s, the International Committee of the Red Cross sponsored a series of international conferences to discuss limitations on "weapons that cause unnecessary suffering or have indiscriminate effects." These conferences have considered proscribing specific weapons, such as cluster and concussion bombs. If, as seems likely, the banning of such weapons is on the agenda of the Special Session of the UN General Assembly on Disarmament scheduled for 1978, their deployment may be curtailed.

CONCLUSION

Will the conventional weapons technologies of the 1980s be more or less stabilizing than the armaments of the 1970s? How many nations will be capable of producing the new weapons of the 1980s?

The problems posed by the arms trade would be reduced greatly if a clear distinction could be drawn between defensive and offensive weapons. If the best defense really were a good defense (instead of a good offense), producer nations could actively promote the transfer of defensive systems and hope that some meaningful restriction on the transfer of offensive weapons might be concluded and honored. Unfortunately no accepted distinction now exists between offense and defense, and the weapon technologies planned for the 1980s will probably blur the distinction even further.

Precision-guided munitions may on balance favor a defensive strategy, but there are so many important qualifications to this generalization that it is worthless as a guide to action. An unfettered international trade in PGMs would not necessarily make the world a more stable and peaceful place. But three general conclusions about new technologies in the 1980s can be advanced.

First, some PGMs will be acquired by a large number of nations. These new weapons are too attractive not to be incorporated into the inventories of many states. Moreover, first-generation PGMs are relatively simple to design and produce. About 15 industrialized nations were capable of producing large numbers of PGMs in the mid-1970s; the number of potential producers can only continue to grow in the years ahead. Any attempt to limit the transfer of less sophisticated PGMs will almost certainly fail. In the unlikely event that such a limitation were observed, it would only stimulate indigenous production.

The second conclusion is that PGMs will probably attenuate the demand for very high-cost, high-performance weapon systems. A $20 million aircraft can be used in combat only when low attrition rates are fairly certain. Such certainty would not exist in a PGM environment. Many nations will want a few fancy weapon systems to satisfy interservice rivalries and considerations of national prestige. But only a few states will be able to afford more than symbolic numbers of such systems. PGMs will increase the attractiveness of low-cost systems that are simple to operate and easy to repair and whose loss in combat would not be catastrophic.

Third, the conventional weapons of the 1980s will very likely increase the rate at which personnel and material will be consumed in combat. The new weapons may not make war more likely, but should war occur, both PGMs and the new area weapons will accelerate the pace and the ferocity of fighting.

The following chart summarizes weapons trends in the 1980s and projected demand for different categories of armament:

61

Weapons Technology	Demand
Precision-guided anti-tank and anti-aircraft missiles	Increasing
High-performance, high-cost systems	Declining
High-attrition, low-cost systems	Increasing

Most of the new weapon technologies that will be transferred in the 1980s are relatively less complex than many systems now being traded. The trend is toward simpler, more durable, and more easily serviced weapons. Future combat aircraft, as well as the new area munitions now under development, will be cheaper, simpler to operate, and easier to maintain than the systems traded in the 1970s. The United States F-16, the French Mirage F-1, the Anglo-Italian-German Multi-Role Combat Aircraft, and the Israeli Kfir—all built with export possibilities clearly in mind—will sell for less than $10 million each. That is less than half the unit cost of the United States F-14. Even high-cost, high-performance systems are becoming easier to repair: the F-15 has about one-fifth the number of serviceable spare parts of the F-4.

At the same time that weapons systems become simpler, more nations will become technically capable of producing weapons indigenously, perhaps for export. The technical trends in evidence in the late 1970s clearly suggest that arms transfers will become increasingly difficult to control in the 1980s.

FIVE

Economic Considerations

A number of economic factors will influence the nature and extent of arms trade in the 1980s. One important question is, Which nations will be the major arms recipients in the coming decade; which countries will have the economic resources and the demand for large purchases of weapons? For potential suppliers, What are the economic justifications of arms transfers? What effect will the technological developments just described have on the arms market of the 1980s?

TRENDS IN THE 1970s

The total value of military hardware transferred in 1975 was $8.9 billion, compared with $5.3 billion in 1965 (constant 1974 United States dollars).[16] Imports by the industrialized nations remained fairly constant over the decade, and virtually the entire increase in United States arms trade was accounted for by the developing nations. In 1975 nearly three-quarters of all arms transfers were to the Third World.

During the first half of the 1970s, the war in Vietnam and the military buildup in the Middle East so dominated arms transac-

[16] *World Military Expenditures and Arms Transfers, 1966–1975,* U.S. Arms Control and Disarmament Agency, Washington, D.C., 1976, p. 56. In addition to excluding *deliveries* after December 31, 1975, these data also exclude training, services, consumables, and construction, estimated to account for an additional 24 percent.

tions that it is difficult to talk about general trends for that period. A few facts need to be stressed. Deliveries to OPEC countries rose from $0.5 billion in 1965 to $1.8 billion (constant 1973 United States dollars) *before* 1973 and thus before the oil embargo and subsequent price increases. Indonesia accounted for nearly one-half of OPEC nations' arms deliveries in 1965 but averaged deliveries of only $18 million per year in the decade thereafter. Iran showed a rapid and steady rise in arms imports beginning in 1965. Deliveries to Iraq, Libya, and Saudi Arabia—the main OPEC arms importers—began to increase only after 1970, but before the 1973 Yom Kippur War and the quadrupling of the price of oil.

Arms imports by Latin America are small in absolute amounts (yearly aveiage between 1965 and 1974 of $264 million constant United States dollars) but increased over 250 percent from 1965 to 1974. The only region showing a downward trend during the past decade was South Asia.

Seventy percent of all *orders* for arms sales between 1973 and 1976 were placed by OPEC and Middle Eastern countries. Thus, *deliveries* to these nations will remain very high into the early 1980s even if no further orders are forthcoming.[17]

Economic Justifications

The main economic justifications for exporting arms stem from two concerns: the overall health of the exporter's national economy and the profitability of defense industries. Table 2 shows the relationship between total exports and military exports for each of the major supplier nations. France and Great Britain are often thought to be the nations most dependent upon arms exports, but by some measures they are much less dependent than the United States and the Soviet Union. It is true, of course, that France and Britain are more generally dependent on exports than either the United States or the Soviet Union. But the ratio of military to civilian exports is higher in the Soviet Union than in any other arms-exporting country. Even for the Soviet Union,

[17]Ibid.

TABLE 2
Comparison of Four Major Military Exporters

	(1) Total Exports (current $ billions)	(2) Exports as Percentage of GNP	(3) Military Exports (current $ billions)	(4) Military Exports as Percentage of Total Exports	(5) Military Exports as Percentage of World Military Exports
1970					
United States	43.251	4.4	3.12	7.2	53.3
Great Britain	19.352	20.0	0.083	0.4	1.4
France	18.098	14.0	0.198	1.1	3.4
Soviet Union	12.8	3.9	1.53	11.95	26.1
1971					
United States	44.136	4.1	3.38	7.7	53.2
Great Britain	22.321	18.5	0.178	0.8	2.8
France	20.751	13.6	0.154	0.7	2.4
Soviet Union	13.806	4.0	1.62	11.7	25.5
1972					
United States	49.787	4.2	4.1	8.2	47.0
Great Britain	24.37	17.9	0.312	1.3	3.6
France	26.451	12.9	0.541	2.0	6.2
Soviet Union	15.409	4.1	2.43	15.8	27.9
1973					
United States	71.347	5.5	5.02	7.0	52.5
Great Britain	30.339	25.0	0.333	1.1	3.5
France	36.659	13.8	0.571	1.6	6.0
Soviet Union	21.332	4.8	2.84	13.3	29.8
1974					
United States	98.524	7.0	4.16	4.2	45.1
Great Britain	38.634	25.0	0.463	1.2	5.0
France	46.46	16.4	0.561	1.2	6.0
Soviet Union	27.374	6.0	2.81	10.3	30.4

TABLE 2
Comparison of Four Major Military Exporters (continued)

	(1) Total Exports (current $ billions)	(2) Exports as Percentage of GNP	(3) Military Exports (current $ billions)	(4) Military Exports as Percentage of Total Exports	(5) Military Exports as Percentage of World Military Exports
1975					
United States	107.6	7.2	4.85	4.5	49.9
Great Britain	44.1	14.2	0.378	0.8	3.9
France	52.9	16.1	0.564	0.9	5.1
Soviet Union	33.36	6.6	2.61	7.8	26.9

SOURCES: International Monetary Fund, *Direction of Trade, 1969–1975, Compendium,* and 1976; Central Intelligence Agency, *Handbook of Economic Statistics,* August 1975, p. 54; Arms Control and Disarmament Agency, *World Military Expenditures and Arms Transfers, 1966–1975; United Nations Statistical Yearbook, 1975,* pp. 433, 554; Department of Commerce, *U.S. Exports 1976;* Economist Intelligence Unit, *Economic Trends: US, USSR, France, Great Britain, 1974–76.*

however, arms exports account for only 10 to 15 percent of total exports.

Table 2 also shows the division of total military exports among the four major suppliers. The United States remains the leading arms exporter, although its share of the total market has declined from 53 percent in 1970 to 50 percent in 1975. The Soviet Union increased its percentage slightly; France went from 3 to 5 percent. Great Britain showed the biggest percentage increase, but remained the smallest of the big four exporters in total volume.

Among the economic benefits that have been ascribed to the arms-export business are the lengthening of production runs, thereby reducing unit costs; the ability to recoup expenses for research and development; increases in domestic employment; the development and maintenance of technological expertise in weapons production; the maintenance of a viable domestic arms industry; and the disposal of surplus or obsolete equipment at better than scrap-material prices.

Studies by the Congressional Budget Office indicate that these domestic economic benefits derived from selling arms abroad, when combined with contracts for services and construction, in effect reduced the actual cost of arms procurement by approximately 7 percent.[18] Assuming a $9 billion sales program (the ceiling suggested by the 94th Congress), the savings would be approximately $630 million a year, or slightly more than one-half of 1 percent of current defense outlays. If similar budgetary savings from arms sales accrued in France and Great Britain, they would amount to $32 million a year for each country (based on 1974 arms deliveries). Department of Labor estimates suggest that arms sales of $9 billion would require about 400,000 jobs in the United States, approximately one-half of 1 percent of total employment.[19]

Looking at the balance of payments, Table 2 reveals that the economic imperative of arms trade from a *national* perspective is not particularly compelling. In 1975 arms exports accounted for between 1 and 10 percent of total exports for each of the four major supplier states. For the Western suppliers, improved balance of payments from increased arms sales were dwarfed by the fourfold rise in the price of oil, estimated to cost the United States alone approximately $20 billion in 1975 and about $30 billion in 1976. Even if France and Great Britain were to double their future arms sales to OPEC countries for the years 1977–1980, these additional sales would be equal to only 7 percent of the increase in their oil-import costs resulting from higher oil prices.[20]

In discussing balance-of-payments difficulties, it is useful to distinguish between short- and long-term effects. Short-term advantages accruing from increased military sales abroad may be partially offset by reductions in purchases of capital equipment and other nonmilitary imports by arms-purchasing states. Ed-

[18]James R. Capra et al., "The Effect of Foreign Military Sales on the Cost of U.S. Weapons," in *Foreign Military Sales and U.S. Weapons Costs*, Staff Working Paper, Congressional Budget Office, Washington, D.C., May 5, 1976.
[19]Cited in Edward R. Fried, *The Economics of Arms Transfers*, draft paper.
[20]Ibid., p. 18.

ward Fried of the Brookings Institution argues that in the event of decreasing United States arms sales to countries like Iran, such countries "would probably spend less in total on arms imports, because other suppliers would not be able to sell either as much, or as sophisticated equipment as Iran is obtaining from the United States."[21] In such a circumstance Iran would probably spend *more* on nonmilitary imports, some of which would be civilian United States products. These increased civilian sales would serve as partial compensation for United States losses from the reduction of its arms exports. These considerations, of course, would not apply to countries with no foreign exchange constraints, such as Saudi Arabia.

In the longer term, increases in United States arms sales (or in any exports) would cause an appreciation of the exchange rate. This strengthening of the United States dollar would eventually reduce exports of nonmilitary goods, a condition that might cause lower employment in nondefense industries. With a fully recovered economy, total United States employment would be approximately the same with or without the increased arms sales. But the relative positions of specific firms and of the military and civilian industrial sectors would be different.[22]

While none of the four main arms supplier nations is heavily dependent upon arms exports, individual industries within each country often are. In France, Great Britain, and the United States, the aerospace industry is most dependent upon military exports. Representatives of the French and British governments claim that their aerospace industries must export at least half of their output in order to survive. The military export share of United States aerospace production is smaller (30 percent) than that of France and Great Britain, although the absolute amount exported is far greater. Several United States firms are substantially dependent on foreign military sales. Bell Helicopter derives 42 percent of its revenue from foreign sales; Northrop, 34 percent; Grumman, 26 percent.[23]

[21]Ibid., p. 13.
[22]Ibid., p. 14.
[23]*Foreign Assistance Authorization, Arms Sales Issues, Hearings before the Subcommittee on Foreign Assistance of the Committee on Foreign Relations*, 94th Cong., 1st Sess., June and November 1975, p. 276.

The British shipbuilding industry is also increasing its dependence upon military exports, rising from 10 percent in 1971 to 38 percent in 1974. For the United States and France, the shipbuilding industry has not been highly dependent upon exports. The percentage of exports for the United States shipbuilding industry fluctuated between 3 and 11 percent from 1971 to 1974. The French percentages varied between 3 and 14 percent for those years.

Arms exports are more important than they appear to be in simple economic terms for a variety of reasons. The British and French view military exports as vital for the continued viability of their national defense production lines. In the United States the major defense exporters often employ large numbers of people, making arms sales an important issue for their representatives in Congress. The defense industries are well represented in Washington through lobbyists, law firms, and trade associations. These political facts of life are unlikely to change appreciably in the coming decade and will provide strong incentives for high levels of arms sales by the major supplier nations.

Arms trade in the 1980s will also be shaped by qualitative changes that began to occur during the latter 1970s. In the industrialized world these included increasing commercialization and the growing desire for weapon standardization.

COMMERCIALIZATION

France has often been cited as the best example of a country whose arms trade policies are determined more by commercial than political motivations. Long before the 1973 energy crisis, the French (and to a lesser extent the British) sought the most lucrative available markets and were largely uninhibited by political restraints. During the mid-1970s, in large part as a result of the need to pay for expensive oil imports, other major Western arms exporters followed the French lead and began paying greater attention to economic considerations. Even for the Soviet Union, the acquisition of hard currency has come to be an important benefit of arms sales, along with the more traditional objectives of access to bases, political influence, and ideological adherence.

For recipient states, the major advantage of growing commercialization has been the diversification of supply. Any nation wanting to buy arms today will find a much larger array of potential suppliers than at any other time. In the 1950s Iran imported arms only from the United States; in the 1970s the Shah had contracts with at least eight different supplier states.

But the trend may also involve some costs and risks for recipients. The new arms exporters may be less reliable than traditional supplier nations that feel some sense of political obligation to the recipient. The airlifts mounted by the Soviet Union and the United States to their respective clients during the Yom Kippur War would almost certainly not have been undertaken if the producers had been interested only in earning money. Nonetheless, commercially minded arms exporters have at times proved reluctant to cut off arms supplies in the face of political embarrassment. The British government stoically maintained its arms shipments to Nigeria during the Biafran civil war despite massive internal and external opposition. Along with the French, the British have also ignored the protestations of nearly every other country in the world on the question of arms sales to South Africa.[24]

Commercialization and diversification of supply reflect a general shift from a bipolar to a multipolar world and a loosening of the alliance-based ties of the cold war era. In the 1970s, arms acquisitions of Third World nations increasingly crossed bloc lines. For example, Rumania and the Yemen Arab Republic, traditional clients of the Soviet Union, ordered arms from the United States; Kuwait demonstrated its independence from the West by ordering some weapons from the Soviet Union. Such cross-bloc acquisitions will continue in the 1980s as many nations seek to follow more independent lines of foreign policy.

Cultivating a number of different arms suppliers, including those across traditional bloc lines, gives recipient nations additional bargaining leverage. The pressure on the United States in 1976 to see that Egypt could find Western sources of weapons and

[24]Leonard Beaton, *Economic Pressures in the Arms Trade*, Occasional Paper, School of International Affairs, Carleton University, Ottawa, Canada, March 1971.

reduce its dependence on the Soviet Union is a good illustration. At the same time, there are major costs involved in changing suppliers, not only during the period of transition but also while trying to maintain disparate equipment in the weapons inventory. Egypt's reliance on Soviet equipment reflected these problems. While major Soviet-built platforms, such as MiG-21, could be refitted with Western engines, the process is time-consuming, difficult, and prohibitively expensive. If different radars were used, the airframes might have to be modified. Many components and support systems would have to switch from Soviet vacuum-tube electronic technology to the West's solid-state equipment, a process that would require retraining a vast number of technicians and mechanics. Many systems, such as surface-to-air missiles, could not be refitted at all, and would have to be dismantled and replaced with new Western missiles if needed spare parts were not available from the Soviet Union.

The desire to keep down production costs by exporting arms and the competition among the industrialized states for petrodollars made the arms trade a buyers' market. But the potential costs of diversifying military supplies cause arms importers to exercise considerable caution. Cross-bloc bargaining will continue in the 1980s, but the recipient nations will have to trade off the advantages that obtain from multiple suppliers with the disadvantages of a nonintegrated defense inventory.

EUROPEAN STANDARDIZATION

Another important arms trade issue for the 1980s will be the question of weapons standardization. The importance of standardized military weaponry within an alliance is obvious: NATO has suffered substantially in the past for its lack of standardization. Politically the alliance has been troubled by competition among member states for weapons contracts; militarily it has been hurt by the inability to interchange different nations' armaments and spare parts. Added to this is the enormous financial waste of many nations maintaining separate research and development programs and production lines. It is often pointed out that although NATO spent more than the Warsaw Pact for

71

armaments from the mid-1960s to the mid-1970s, the decade saw a greater qualitative and quantitative improvement in Warsaw Pact equipment. This shift was in large part a result of NATO's lack of standardization. Through the mid-1970s the variety of weapons in NATO inventories actually increased: diversification outstripped efforts at standardization. In the mid-1970s the NATO alliance used 4 different main battle tanks, 31 separate anti-tank weapons, and 20 different types of aircraft. The ammunition used by Dutch, British, and German ships was not interchangeable.[25]

The arguments for increased standardization are compelling, but the obstacles are formidable. Thus the prognosis for standardization within NATO is mixed. The United States has conceded that standardization cannot be achieved simply by requiring the European members to buy American weapons. There must be a "two-way street" of arms purchases between the United States and Europe. The 1976 competition for a new main battle tank provided an opportunity to test American sincerity on this point. Despite an earlier announcement that the United States would purchase the German Leopard tank if it proved superior to two American prototypes, the Army selected one of the American models before its evaluation of the German tank was completed.[26] Despite this setback, some standardization of tank design was accomplished. A strong effort was made to incorporate as many standard components as possible in the American and German tanks. Both are to be powered by the same gas turbine engine and will use the same track system.

There are some indications that by the second half of the 1980s, there will be significant improvements in NATO standardization. Encouraging developments include the agreement between the Netherlands and West Germany to standardize as far as possible the new frigate each is building, joint design of a new coastal submarine by Norway and West Germany, the U.S. Army's purchase of the Franco-German Roland II missile system, and France's willingness to join the Independent Program Group

[25]Norman L. Dodd, "Standardization in NATO," *National Defense*, vol. 60, November-December 1975, pp. 210–213.

[26]See John Finney, "U.S. Weighing Use of a German Tank," *New York Times*, February 13, 1976, and "Army Picks Chrysler to Develop a New Tank at $4.9 Billion Cost," *New York Times*, November 13, 1976.

(IPG), an informal unit formed within NATO to increase European arms sales to the United States. These developments are in addition to ongoing standardization programs by NATO countries, including seven aircraft, seven missiles, a hydrofoil missile boat, and a main battle tank.[27]

There are various forms of standardization: commonality, interoperability, interchangeability, and compatibility. In the 1970s, common user items included only maps, fuels, medical supplies, and small-arms ammunition. By the late 1980s, this category will include torpedoes, gas turbine engines for naval ships, helicopters, and short-range missiles. Commonality affords opportunities for sharing training, maintenance, and exercises.

Interoperable equipment consists primarily of electronics communication systems, such as the NATO Air Defense Ground Environment stretching from Norway to Turkey. The system consists of 80 radar sites and a number of computers, all using the same language, symbols, and software.[28] The 1976 Defense Appropriation Authorization Act expressed the sense of the U.S. Congress that military equipment for United States forces stationed in Europe should be made interoperable with other NATO members to the maximum extent feasible.

Interchangeability of parts in vehicles, tanks, guns, and aircraft is also becoming much more common. Both within NATO (Netherlands) and outside NATO (Switzerland), there is growing specialization in particular components, such as radars and fire control systems, that can be incorporated into complete weapons systems.

Compatibility reduces the danger of interference with communications, guidance, and similar electronics systems. The lack of common radio frequencies, codes for data transmission, and systems for identifying friend or foe in the late 1970s raises the serious danger of friendly aircraft being inadvertently shot down.[29]

[27]*SIPRI Yearbook 1975*, Stockholm International Peace Research Institute, 1975, p. 149.

[28]Gardiner Tucker, "Standardization and the Joint Defense," *NATO Review*, no. 1, January 1, 1975, pp. 10–14.

[29]Dodd, "Standardization in NATO."

In analyzing European-American cooperation in the 1980s, a useful distinction can be drawn between weapon platforms and the systems placed on those platforms—between aircraft, tanks, and ships, on the one hand, and the ordnance that such platforms carry, on the other. The expense and high level of technical expertise required to produce combat aircraft make it highly likely that the United States will continue to dominate that area of the NATO market. For the armaments placed on the platforms, prospects are for a greater share of the market going to the West Europeans as compensation for the dominance of the United States in the production of platforms. Many of the new weapons that will enter NATO inventories during the 1980s can be produced by several European countries. PGMs, air-scatterable mines, anti-personnel cluster-bomb units, and fuel-air explosives can all be produced without prohibitively high investment costs. The large numbers of each missile produced—in the tens of thousands—mean that production lines will be long enough to enable the Europeans to compete with the Americans on these low-cost, high-technology items.

The French Exocet anti-ship missile is already entering service with the French, British, and German navies, and eight other countries have placed orders for it. France, which is currently stressing the production of missiles, may well be the primary beneficiary of the new two-tiered system of NATO standardization.

The 1980s may bring a stretching out of the production lines of weapon platforms in response to the expected continuing rapid development of second- and third-generation weapons to be mounted on the platforms. As the armaments develop longer range and increased speed, later models of the platforms will be modified to match better the weapons' improved capabilities.

Another method for analyzing European standardization in the 1980s is to differentiate between intra-European collaboration and cooperation between the United States and its European allies. The intra-European goal will be to divide development and production among the countries in approximate proportion to their requirements for the product and their financial contribution. This is the principle of *juste retour*. Final assembly of the components will usually occur in each participating country. The recent four-nation (Germany, Belgium, the Netherlands, and Denmark) NATO consortium arrangement on the F-16 may well set a pattern for similar arrangements in the 1980s.

One of the most noteworthy features of the NATO competition for a new lightweight fighter was that each of the three major bidders—Sweden's Viggen, France's F-1, and the United States' F-16—offered substantial inducements to the prospective buyers. These incentives ranged from 35 percent of the value of each French F-1 produced to be manufactured by the four purchasing states to more than 50 percent for each Swedish Viggen. Viggen also promised $1.2 billion in nonaeronautical investments over the next 10 years in the form of Saab auto and Volvo truck plants to be built in the European buyer countries. The United States F-16, winner of the competition, will entail 40 percent co-production on the 348 planes produced for the consortium, 10 percent co-production of the 650 ordered by the U.S. Air Force and 15 percent co-production of all F-16s produced for export outside NATO.[30]

The United States contract will be a dual-source scheme, meaning that each component produced in the four-nation NATO consortium is being produced in the United States in approximately equal numbers. The presumed advantages of this arrangement are that the competition between the manufacturers may result in lower prices and that the entire program will be less vulnerable to unforeseen events in either the United States or in the four European purchasing states. In contrast, the Viggen and F-1 programs were single-source plans, in which the components produced in the four countries would not be produced elsewhere. The advantages here are the usual benefits of longer production lines—lower per-unit cost, with nonrecurring costs written off over a larger series and a greater "learning curve" effect.

In summary, NATO standardization in the 1980s is likely to be two-tiered, with American preponderance in the major weapons platforms and increasing European collaboration in tactical missiles and other armaments. Disputes over standardization within the alliance will no doubt continue throughout the 1980s, since the

[30]Robert R. Ropelieski, "NATO Consortium Expects Satisfactory F-16 Offsets," *Aviation Week and Space Technology*, vol. 104, no. 8, February 23, 1976, pp. 17–18.

United States will retain an inherent advantage in high-technology, high-cost systems. But other NATO members will become increasingly competitive in new areas of technology. Based on the co-production promises extended in the 1970s, extensive co-production rights will become integral components of all large European purchases of major weapons in the 1980s.

The impact of increased NATO standardization on arms sales to the developing nations is not likely to be significant in the 1980s. The United States market, whose current procurement is approximately $30 billion, is potentially several times as large as the combined arms market of all the developing nations. In theory, the United States could perhaps persuade its European allies to forego some of their Third World markets in exchange for a guaranteed share of the United States market. But is such a proposal practical? Would the United States simply inform a former French or British client that it was now that country's new arms supplier? Or would the United States and the French or British jointly try to convince that recipient nation that it really did not have a defense requirement for the new weapon? Both alternatives seem highly improbable. Nor does it appear to be in the best interests of the United States to become the sole supplier of arms to many developing nations. In practical terms, European standardization will not in itself result in major changes in arms trading between developed and developing nations—with the possible exception being that specialization of defense production within NATO will decrease the number of alternative systems available for sale.

LICENSING AGREEMENTS AND INDIGENOUS PRODUCTION IN DEVELOPING NATIONS

The major changes in the arms trade patterns of developing nations that may occur in the 1980s will result from greatly increased indigenous production. In contrast to the growing willingness of the industrial nations to give up some political independence in order to compete in a buyer's market, the dominant impulse of developing nations' plans for the coming decade is toward arms independence. First and foremost among the pressures for indigenous production is a desire to reduce dependence for spare parts and replacements. Uncertainty regarding the commitments of suppliers spurs the drive for indigenous production. It is not surprising that the nations pushing their own defense production most vigorously are India, Israel, South Africa, South Korea, and Taiwan. Other motivations for indigenous production include the need to reduce foreign exchange outflows, to support local industry, and to attain the prestige attached to modern production capabilities. While nearly one-third of the developing nations now produce some of their own small arms and ammunition, total self-sufficiency in weaponry will continue to be illusory for all but a few nations.

Third World countries can acquire weapons in several ways ranging from outright importation, to assembly of subsets, to assembly of components, to licensed production, to indigenous design using imported components, to collaborative production projects, and finally, to wholly indigenous development and production. A first step along the long road to indigenous production is to build repair and overhaul facilities for the maintenance of imported weapons. India and Israel took this step in the 1950s; Iran is currently following this path.

The first phase in a licensed production program usually involves only local assembly of prefabricated parts imported from the licensing nation. This initial step is often accompanied by considerable technical assistance from the licenser. Delays and bottlenecks can result if such help is not forthcoming. Even when the technical assistance is forthcoming, success is not assured. In 1960 a local missile industry was initiated in Egypt under the guidance of the German rocket expert W. Pilz, a former associate of Werner von Braun. By 1962 there were 250 West German rocket experts and technicians in Egypt, yet in 1969 the entire project disintegrated and was abolished. The failure was due to Egypt's inability to train local personnel to work with and eventually take over from the foreign experts. A trained and skilled work force is essential for autonomous local production.

Indigenous production frequently turns out to be more expensive than originally estimated and is sometimes even more expensive than buying the complete weapon abroad.[31] The costs of research and development are often underestimated, and the costs of materials increase as the proportion of indigenous to imported material rises and preferential costs are paid to domestic producers. The prices of components tend to be relatively high in proportion to the price of the complete weapon, so that the importation of components becomes very expensive. The lack of testing facilities within the country also increases the cost if the test trials have to be undertaken elsewhere.

Instead of creating independence, indigenous production usually creates a new set of dependencies. Most often the machinery, the patents, and the high-technology components all have to be imported. Even China, the only country independent of foreign suppliers of components for its domestic weapons projects, imported more than $200 million worth of electronic equipment during 1960–1970. Israel's Kfir fighter-bomber is powered by a General Electric–licensed engine that is assembled in Israel with about 60 percent of the parts built in Israel and 40 percent imported from the United States. Argentinian planes use engines imported from France, and India's MiG-21, seven years after it was first produced, still was more Russian- than Indian-made.[32]

Sales of license-produced weapons also depend on the resale regulations of the original supplier. The United States requires controls on the re-export of products incorporating American technology or components. The Soviet Union successfully prevented India from supplying Egypt with spare parts for MiG-21 jet fighters because the Soviet-Indian MiG-21 licensing agreement barred the sale of equipment to third countries. But the Soviet Union was unable to prevent China from transferring 30 engines from its Soviet-licensed MiG-17s and MiG-21s to Egypt in 1975.[33]

[31]*SIPRI Yearbook 1973*, Stockholm International Peace Research Institute, 1973, pp. 350–356.

[32]*Aviation Week and Space Technology*, December 15, 1975, p. 11. See also Dennis Childs and Michael Kidron, "India, the USSR and the MiG Project," *Economic and Political Weekly* (Bombay), vol. 8, no. 38, September 22, 1973.

[33]"India Confirms Ban on Parts for Egypt," *New York Times*, March 18, 1976; "Sadat Says He Got 30 Jet Engines from China," *Boston Globe*, March 26, 1976.

To some extent, the success or failure of indigenous production depends on what one expects from the process. Israel, a country often held up as a model of successful domestic production, started from a high technological skill base, is indeed producing about 30 percent of its weaponry needs, and is said to be self-sufficient in small arms, bombs, explosives, unguided rockets, and ammunition.[34] Israel is now producing domestically developed high-performance combat aircraft, light trainers, missile systems, STOL military transports, medium tanks, armored cars, missile boats, electronics and avionics, and a comprehensive range of tactical communications equipment.[35]

The Israeli Aircraft Industries is reported to have doubled export sales yearly, from approximately $45 million in 1975 to $90 million in 1976 and $200 million in 1977. The prime marketing targets for the Kfir fighter are South America, Southeast Asia, and Africa. Israel is offering a worldwide service backup for its Kfir sales and is planning to license production of the plane in South Africa, Peru, and Venezuela. But despite these sorts of activities, Israel will probably not succeed in achieving more than 50 percent self-sufficiency in the 1980s and will remain dependent on the United States for most of its major weapon platforms.

Three changes in licensed and indigenous production are likely to occur in the 1980s:

1. *More nations will be able to achieve weapons independence by indigenous production.* Many nations are developing a strong industrial base that will enable them to handle licensed production. Taiwan, South Korea, and South Africa are prime examples. Japan is already producing or developing indigenous supersonic aircraft, main battle tanks, and submarines.

   In the 1980s such countries will be more independent vis-à-vis the major arms suppliers than they are today. However, most countries will likely remain dependent on the superpowers for such front-line weapon platforms as high-performance combat aircraft.

[34]*SIPRI Yearbook 1975*, p. 196, and Irvine J. Cohen, "Israeli Defense Capability," *National Defense*, vol. 60, January/February 1976, pp. 271–273.
[35]Cohen, "Israeli Defense Capability," pp. 271–273.

TABLE 3

Licensed Production of Major Weapon Systems and Use of Foreign Components in Indigenous Design, 1950–1974*

Suppliers	Argentina	Brazil	Egypt	India	Indonesia	Israel	Pakistan	Philippines	South Africa	Taiwan
France										
Aircraft	1,3	3		1,3		1	3		3	
Tanks	2								1,3	
Ships										
Missiles		3		2,3		1,2				
Components	1,2,3	2,3	3	1,2,3		1,2			3	
Great Britain										
Aircraft		3	3	1,2,3						
Tanks				2						
Ships		3		2				3		
Missiles										
Components	1,2,3	1,2,3		1,2,3		1			1,2,3	
Soviet Union										
Aircraft				1,3						

Tanks		3					
Ships							
Missiles	1,3						
Components	1,3						
United States							
Aircraft	1,2,3				3	3	2,3
Tanks		1		1			
Ships					3		
Missiles				3			
Components	1,2,3	1,2,3	1	2,3	3	3	2,3
West Germany							
Aircraft		2			3	3	
Tanks				3	3		
Ships	2,3		3	3			1
Missiles					3		1
Components		2	3	3	3	3	

*"1" means 1950–1964; "2" means 1965–1969; "3" means 1970–1974. The date used for licensed production of major weapons systems is the year the licensing agreement was signed. The date used for indigenous design is the year production began. *Foreign components* refers to parts, such as engines, that were obtained from a foreign supplier, even though the weapon system itself is of indigenous design. The foreign components for an indigenous design may either be produced locally under a licensing agreement or be purchased directly from abroad.

SOURCES: *Arms Trade with the Third World*, SIPRI, Stockholm, 1971; *SIPRI Yearbooks 1972, 1973, 1974, 1975*; *Jane's Fighting Ships, 1972–73*, London, 1972.

2. *The present trend toward licensed production will accelerate.*
Table 3 depicts the spread of licensed technology in 10 developing countries between 1950 and 1974. Between 1970 and
1974 these nations had signed 47 licensed production agreements with the industrialized world, compared with 27 such
arrangements in force during 1950–1954. The sale of licenses
can be almost as lucrative as the sale of hardware: the same
economic pressures that are loosening political strictures
about sales will, in the 1980s, apply to licensing procedures as
well. France, which now grants licenses for the widest range of
weapons to the largest number of recipients, will be followed
by the other major arms exporters. The Soviet Union, which
currently licenses production only in India, is unlikely to
broaden its licensing activities enough to stay competitive with
the West.

3. *Licensed production of the new technologies will be widespread.* Some of the new technologies, such as first-generation
PGMs and area weapons, are very conducive to licensed
production. The severe and long-lasting dependencies created
by licensed production of supersonic aircraft will be absent in
these systems. However, as production of PGMs advances
into second- and third-generation weapons, developing nations will once again face dependence upon the licensing
countries.

SIX

Demands for Weapons in the 1980s

The dominant factor influencing the nature and dimensions of arms trade in the 1980s will be the demand for arms. Which countries will have both the economic resources and the perceived need for large purchases? Will the major purchasers of the 1980s be the same big arms customers of the 1970s? Which other countries are likely to be large purchasers in the next decade? What general propositions can be made about the demand side of the arms trade equation in the 1980s?

The nations that ordered the most weapons in 1974–75 were Iran, Israel, Libya, Saudi Arabia, and Egypt.[36] We consider first their possible arms expenditures in the 1980s.

Iran

A few years ago Iran was extolled as a developing country that had achieved self-sustaining rapid growth. Scant attention was paid to its high illiteracy, low agricultural productivity, and lack of entrepreneurial-managerial capability.

Forecasts of Iran's economic status in the 1980s have become progressively less optimistic. The Hudson Institute predicts that

[36]*Foreign Assistance Authorization: Arms Sale Issues*, pp. 17–21; *The Military Balance, 1975–1976,* International Institute for Strategic Studies, London, 1975, pp. 89–93; Roger Pajak, Roundtable Discussion, "The Military Balance in the Middle East," 17th Annual Convention, International Studies Association, Toronto, February 28, 1976.

"Iran's economy in 1985, *even on the best projections*, remains not much beyond what India's will be in ten years, and possibly equal to or just behind Mexico's."[37] Iran's revenues from oil exports are expected to peak in 1978 and fall off rather significantly after that. Already Iran is facing balance-of-payments and liquidity problems.

What effect will this have on Iran's arms purchases in the 1980s? Indications are that the Iranian government has already begun to cut back on purchases of arms. For example, two of the six Spruance-class destroyers ordered from the United States will probably be canceled, and lengthy delays are preventing the signing of contracts for the construction of a $2 billion naval base at Chahbahar. Another constraint on Iranian arms orders in the 1980s will simply be the problem of absorbing the billions of dollars of arms ordered in the 1970s. A Senate Foreign Relations Committee report in 1976 stated that "Iran will not be able to absorb and operate within the next five to ten years a large proportion of the sophisticated military systems it has purchased from the United States unless increasing numbers of American personnel go to Iran in a support capacity."[38]

Politically the major factors affecting Iran's demand for weapons in the 1980s—the relationship between Iran and its neighbors, the question of succession to the Shah, and Iran's possible ambitions for hegemony in the Persian Gulf area—are subject to considerable uncertainty.

Israel

Israel's arms imports in the 1980s will depend upon the presence or absence of hostilities, the level of arms expended if hostilities occur, the arms inventories of its perceived opponents, and the production capacity of its indigenous defense industry. Almost all equipment developed for the Israel defense forces is licensed for

[37] Frederick Langer, *Iran: Oil Money and the Ambitions of a Nation*, Hudson Special Report, Hudson Institute, Croton-on-Hudson, N.Y., March 1, 1975.

[38] *U. S. Military Sales to Iran*, Staff Report to the Subcommittee on Foreign Assistance, Committee on Foreign Relations, U.S. Senate, July 1976.

export; frequently export licenses are issued as soon as the domestic production lines are opened.

The Israelis are likely to acquire the following major systems in the 1980s: the F-16, as the follow-on to the F-4, Mirage, and Kfir; new-generation tanks; second- and third-generation PGMs; and a new armored personnel carrier designed to serve as a combat vehicle. The major asymmetries in manpower existing between Israel and the Arab states mean that Israel will have to move toward more fire-intensive systems—that is, in effect, greater firepower per capita.

Israel will probably not be able to revert to paying cash for most of its weapons imports, as was predominantly the case prior to 1967. But whether Israel receives most of its imports in the form of grants or low-interest credits, it will remain a major arms importer in the 1980s.

Libya

Libya until very recently was a modest importer of arms. Increased oil revenues and revolutionary fervor have been major factors in the steadily increasing rate of arms acquisitions, culminating in a $2 billion order signed with the Soviet Union in 1974. The unpredictable nature of the Egyptian-Libyan rift and the uncertain duration of the alliance between fervently anti-Communist Libya and the Soviet Union, as well as the vagaries of Colonel Qaddafi, make forecasts of future Libyan arms purchases tenuous at best. Libya's oil reserves will sustain production of 2 million barrels per day through 1990. Oil revenues will enable Libya to indulge its preference for Western technology and to enhance its independence through diversified sources of arms supplies.

Saudi Arabia

Most of the difficulties that loom large for the Iranian economy in 1985 do not threaten Saudi Arabia. Simply stated, Saudi Arabia has so much oil and so small a population that during the 1980s it will become increasingly prosperous and able to purchase weapons. The Institute for Strategic Studies estimates that Saudi military spending increased more than threefold from 1974 to 1975, and that it will total $30 billion over the period 1975–1980.[39]

Bottlenecks and labor shortages impose some limitations on Saudi Arabia's ability to purchase weapons. Currently only two Saudi ports can offload material and equipment. Delays of four to six weeks are common. With a population of about 4.5 million and a literacy rate of less than 25 percent, Saudi Arabia also faces severe manpower shortages at all levels, especially in middle-management and skilled technical positions. These factors will not limit the Saudis' ability to purchase arms, but they will restrict the ability to absorb new weapons, a fact that will be reflected in future purchase orders.

Saudi oil reserves (estimated at over 150 billion barrels) will provide revenues in the 1980s to acquire whatever arms the leaders choose, subject to the problems of absorption. Given these parameters and assuming internal stability, as exemplified in the smooth transition from Faisal to Khalid in 1974, Saudi arms imports in the 1980s may well remain large by pre-1972 standards, but will have leveled off considerably from their surge of the mid-1970s.

Egypt

Egypt's defense spending has increased to over one-third of its GNP. Currently in the process of changing arms suppliers, Cairo has projected a need for arms aid of at least $5 to $7 billion over the next 10 years. As the real problems of changing suppliers become apparent, they could well result in a significant increase or at least a continued high level of imports to maintain operational inventories at reasonable levels. Egypt's economic ability to acquire the technically sophisticated weapons it desires will depend on the willingness of its oil-rich allies to finance them or on the willingness of its suppliers to furnish the arms free of charge.

[39]International Institute for Strategic Studies, *The Military Balance, 1975–1976*, London, 1976.

86

Politically, Egypt's demand for arms will depend upon the course of "normalization" of relations with Israel. Three alternative futures can be projected. In the first, gradual but perceptible normalization would slowly lead to reductions in the rate of arms acquisitions. The second would be a continuation of the present situation: a peaceful but heavily armed coexistence with continued high rates of arms purchases on both sides. The third alternative would be recurrent outbreaks of hostilities, ensuring even higher demands for weapon replacements.[40]

Countries that were not major arms purchasers in the 1970s but may become so in the 1980s include South Africa and Brazil.

South Africa

South Africa has strong economic potential and rapidly rising armaments expenditures. Its major stumbling block to continued economic growth clearly is the increasing level of international isolation and the struggle for black majority rule. South Africa has substantial reserves of several scarce materials—manganese, chromium, platinum, and uranium—and also holds an estimated 60 percent of the gold that can be mined throughout the world.

Despite the UN resolution banning all "sales and shipments of arms, ammunition and vehicles" and "all equipment and materials needed for the manufacture and maintenance of arms and ammunition," South Africa is by far Africa's largest weapons importer south of the Sahara. Britain and the United States have continued to supply spare parts and ammunition; France has not observed the embargo at all and is South Africa's largest source of weapons. Most European countries and the United States have helped to build up South Africa's indigenous production capabilities. South Africa now claims self-sufficiency in meeting all of its arms needs except for warships and long-range aircraft. If racial violence erupts in the 1980s, South Africa may become a real "pariah" state and be forced to rely entirely upon its own

[40]Discussed by Paul Jabber in *Oil, The Arab-Israel Dispute and the Industrial World*, J. C. Hurewitz (ed.), Westview Press, Boulder, Colo., 1976.

production facilities. Short of the outbreak of overt hostilities, South Africa can be expected to be a major element in arms transfers in the 1980s.

Brazil

Brazil's economic potential for satisfying a substantial arms appetite should remain strong through the next decade. The country is rich in natural resources, especially in those extractive minerals that will increase in value as the demands of electrical, nuclear, and advanced materials industries continue to expand. These will be important both to Brazil's own expanding economy and to her role as an exporter of essential raw materials.

The political situation, which appears to be the most important element in Brazilian development, appears fairly stable. Geisel's policy of *distensao*—the increasing participation of nonmilitary sectors in policy formation—has strengthened his base of support. And while he hopes to cut imports 15 percent from 1975 levels in an effort to reduce the trade deficit, arms sales to Brazil can be expected to remain strong in the medium and long run because of internal and regional rivalries.

CONCLUDING PROPOSITIONS

The seven countries discussed in this section differ widely in the military threats they face, and in their natural resources, size, population, and prospects for economic development. It is difficult to draw generalizations from such disparities, but four general proposals seem to emerge from this analysis.

Proposition 1: High-cost weapon inventories of industrialized nations will have to shrink In the United States, it is estimated that the prices of new weapons systems increase by an order of magnitude every 20 years. World military expenditures, expressed in constant dollars, have risen approximately 3 percent annually since 1960.[41] Unless the defense budgets of indus-

---

[41]Sivard, *World Military and Social Expenditures*, 1976, p. 6.

trialized nations grow at unprecedented rates in the future, it would seem that one-for-one replacement of major weapons systems is ruled out. With regard to high-cost weapon platforms, there will have to be either fewer different types of ships, aircraft, and tanks or fewer units of each type.

Proposition 2: Low-cost, high-technology weapon inventories will expand This proposition is likely to hold true for both industrialized and developing nations. Given the low cost of first-generation PGMs, widespread diffusion of such weapons will occur in the 1980s. As both speed and range are improved, the prices will rise rather markedly and the demand for the later models of PGMs in most developing countries will decline accordingly.

Proposition 3: Some developing countries will still have absorption problems Third World countries differ widely on what they are acquiring in their buying spree of the 1970s. For instance, Iran allocated 80 percent of its military imports for hardware, 17 percent for logistics and supply, and 2 percent for training. Between 1974 and 1975 the Shah ordered 400 warplanes, 500 helicopters, 730 tanks, 18 warships, and thousands of missiles.[42] The rapid acquisition of such large quantities of weapons could cause logistics problems even in many developed countries that have a large pool of skilled technicians, good communications and transportation networks, and ready access to ports of entry. In Iran, the absorption of so much hardware will cause severe "digestive" problems well into the 1980s. Orders of military hardware may therefore have reached their apogee before the end of this decade, and the 1980s may be a period of absorption of existing inventories.

On the other hand, Saudi Arabia apportioned only 20 percent of its military imports in hardware and devoted 64 percent to military construction in the 1970s. Since the Saudis are spending this decade trying to build up an infrastructure, we would expect that in the 1980s they will turn to building up their weapons inventories.

[42]Michael T. Klare, "Hoist with Our Own Pahlavi," *The Nation,* vol. 222, no. 4, January 31, 1976, pp. 110–114.

Proposition 4: The 1980s will see the emergence of a new corps of "white-collar mercenaries" These new mercenaries will sell their engineering and managerial expertise rather than traditional military skills.[43] It is estimated that by 1980 there will be 150,000 Americans in Iran associated in some way with servicing the Iranian military forces. By comparison, there were only 238,000 troops in the entire Iranian military establishment in 1974–1975. We expect the same cross-bloc phenomena we observed in the 1970s regarding arms purchases to occur in the 1980s with regard to hiring these experts. Socialist nations, while denouncing capitalism, will be eager to hire radar or communications experts from Rockwell International or pilots from Grumman or systems analysts from Arthur D. Little. And the "politically neutral" experts will be glad to go wherever their services are desired. This trend has already begun and can be expected to accelerate in the 1980s.[44]

[43]Ibid.

[44]Ann Crittenden, "Apolitical American Consultants," *New York Times*, September 28, 1975.

SEVEN

Conclusions and Recommendations

As we have stated throughout this essay, there are very few predictions about arms trade which can be offered with high confidence, owing to uncertainty not only about future trends but also about how such trends will affect one another. In this chapter we will outline several plausible futures for arms trade in the 1980s. We have used judgment, speculation, and intuition in developing this future. We will also identify some alternative but less plausible futures for arms trade.

LIKELY FUTURES

The availability of precision-guided munitions will represent the most notable change in conventional weaponry from the 1970s. In the years ahead, trade in PGMs will almost certainly become increasingly vigorous. One reason to expect a lively trade in such munitions is that perhaps 15 to 20 nations will become capable of producing their own PGMs, and thus of marketing first-generation precision-guided weapons.

The international appetite for high-cost, low-attrition combat aircraft such as the F-14 will diminish significantly by the 1980s. This reduced demand will result in part because these aircraft are too costly to risk in combat against PGMs, but also because ultrasophisticated military systems have proved themselves to be prohibitively expensive, difficult to operate, and hard to service in combat. Producer nations as well as consumers are moving away from latest-state-of-the-art systems to relatively low-cost, high-attrition aircraft such as the F-16, the Mirage F-1, the Saab Viggen, and the Israeli Kfir.

The dominant suppliers of armaments in the 1980s are likely to remain the United States and the Soviet Union. The political and economic factors that account for their predominance are unlikely to change significantly in the decade ahead. In the competition for such relatively high unit-cost items as combat aircraft, other producers will find it increasingly difficult to stay competitive with the superpowers. The 1980s will see a further weakening, and perhaps even the demise, of autonomous European production lines for combat aircraft. European industries will turn more and more to co-production and licensing arrangements with American aircraft industries.

One prediction that can be made with reasonably high confidence is that there will not be another perturbation in international arms trade in the 1980s as dramatic as the one that occurred during the early and mid-1970s. The fantastic rise in arms trade at that time was the result of several unusual factors; such a combination is unlikely to occur again. It is even possible that Iran and other OPEC nations may not have the hard currency required to pay for all of the military equipment they ordered in the 1970s. The first default by an OPEC nation on an arms sale may damp the enthusiasm of producer nations for future transactions.

In any event, it must be remembered that the big jump in arms trade recorded in the years 1973–1975 was in *orders placed*. Major *deliveries* of equipment did not begin until the late 1970s and will continue through the 1980s. The major purchasers of arms in the mid-1970s—Iran and Saudi Arabia—have already bought most of their main-line military forces for the 1980s. Thus they will have no pressing need for major purchases of new equipment until the late 1980s.

The weapons recipients of the 1980s are more difficult to identify than the suppliers. It is very likely that the oil-producing nations will continue to account for a substantial portion of world arms trade. Even with some diminution in OPEC spending power in the coming years, the oil-rich nations will be among the privileged few with substantial reserves of hard currency. The developing nations of Africa and Latin America have traditionally relied upon aid, credits, and preferential prices in order to acquire their armaments. As weapons producers come to see arms transfers more in economic and less in ideological terms, such favored treatment is less likely to occur. The U.S. Congress reflected this shift in attitude by cutting off all military grant aid after September 30, 1977.

The nations of the developing world generally spend a smaller proportion of their GNP on weapons than do the industrialized states. Nearly all the developing countries outside the Middle East devote less than 5 percent of their GNP to armaments. This percentage has increased in recent years and may continue to rise in the 1980s as the developing countries see deliveries of armaments to OPEC countries increasing. But even if the defense burden in such nations does rise, it will continue to account for a relatively small portion of the world arms trade.

What will be the rules—implicit or explicit—of the international arms trade in the 1980s? It is difficult to perceive any general tendencies, much less any faithfully observed rules, that now govern the current world arms trade. Future developments will not make it any easier to develop such guidelines. The United States and other producers will probably continue to examine arms transfers on an ad hoc basis, deciding most cases on their individual merits.

There has never been a clear distinction between offensive and defensive weapons, and the technologies of the coming decade will not help to clarify the difference. Precision-guided munitions, for example, do not unambiguously favor the offense or the defense. Combat aircraft are inherently difficult to categorize. The Northrop F-5 fighter was deliberately designed to be a defensive short-range combat aircraft, but subsequent design improvements extended the range and increased the firepower of the aircraft, making it more suitable for offensive uses. The latest model, the F-5E, has substantial offensive as well as defensive capabilities.

The major arms producers will probably continue to observe the implicit ban on the transfer of nuclear weapons and intercon-

93

tinental delivery systems such as ICBMs and heavy bombers. But another new technology—the cruise missile—will increasingly blur the distinction between tactical and strategic forces. Even at present, every nation with a commerical airliner has a rudimentary long-range strategic capability. The 1980s will probably see more trade in "threshold" items that will further blur the already vague distinctions between offense and defense, strategic and tactical, nuclear and conventional.

Another change that may affect international arms trade in the 1980s is a shift in public and governmental attitudes toward arms trade itself. There may be a greater willingness on the part of many producer nations to sell weapons abroad, particularly if they see their reluctance as only serving to benefit other less scrupulous suppliers. The "high-technology, high-morality" nations, such as Germany and Japan, may well become more actively involved in the arms trade of the future. But this development is not inevitable. The Swedes appear steadfast in their high-morality posture. In France, as noted earlier, the Catholic Church achieved some success in rousing public awareness of the government's nonrestrictive arms trade policy.

This rather gloomy picture is our vision of the most likely future for conventional arms trade. There are, however, a number of other possible if somewhat less likely scenarios.

OTHER FUTURES

One possibility would be a completely free market system for the international transfer of armaments. Changing perceptions of arms trade may reinforce the willingness of many producers to sell their arms with fewer and fewer restrictions. The rules of the arms trade game are fragile enough at present; they depend on maintaining a weak consensus among the major producers. It is possible that a current producer state such as France could adopt a policy of selling to all comers. It is more likely that an emerging industrial state such as Brazil would agree to sell its weapons to all other developing nations (except, of course, to its own neighbors). Trade in what we have called threshold systems may even erode the strongest existing rule of the game, the proscription against trade in strategic nuclear-related systems.

An absolute laissez faire system for arms trade is unlikely. Many nations will refuse to sell some arms to any other state; it is inconceivable, for example, that the United States would sell a nuclear weapon in the 1980s—no matter who the prospective recipient. Most nations will also refuse to sell any weapons to some buyers, for reasons of either ideology or security.

Another possible future for arms trade is a condominium of industrialized nations. The major arms producers could implicitly divide the world into areas in which each producer would have exclusive domain. Each producer would then be permitted to sell only to its own client states. Each producer would also be responsible for maintaining military stability in the region it supplied. Such an arrangement, if it could be implemented, might increase the prospects for regional stability and reduce the risk that major powers would be drawn into a conflict brought about by their client states.

A variant of this future would be a Soviet-American condominium in the arms trade. Conceivably the United States could undercut all other industrialized arms producers and divide the arms trade world with the Soviet Union. Together the two nations could manage international traffic in armaments.

A final—and remote—possibility is complete United States hegemony in world arms trade. Outside Eastern Europe, where the Soviet Union will inevitably remain the major arms supplier, it is conceivable that the United States could run all the other arms producers out of the market. The United States has the strongest military-industrial complex in the world, and despite their rather poor reputation at home, American defense industries have the best research and development in the world and can provide the best military equipment at the lowest cost. In addition, the United States enjoys an excellent reputation as an arms supplier. The United States emphasizes the development of military infrastructure as part of its arms deals; it also is a reliable supplier of spare parts. In contrast, the Soviet Union has an unimpressive record as an arms supplier. Its emphasis on military hardware rather than infrastructure and training may please recipient states in the short run, but such a policy creates serious problems in the long run. Egyptian President Anwar Sadat's disaffection with the Soviet Union as an arms patron is but one example of a familiar pattern.

In a sense, this last future—United States hegemony—is quite close to the first alternative, unrestricted arms trade. Both can come about only if the United States is willing to couple its marketing advantages with a willingness to abandon all of its restraints on the international sale of arms. That prospect appears to be highly unlikely.

Arms Trade and Economic Policy

The economic justifications for arms trade have long been accepted at face value without any serious examination of their validity. What are the imported resources utilized by the supplier countries to produce weapons for export? How likely are arms importers to raise the prices of their raw materials to pay for the increasing cost of their weapons? How much is worldwide inflation intensified as a result of such pressures? The United States defense industry needs to operate on a sound basis, reflecting its own defense needs and not becoming dependent on foreign sales. Economic rationales for arms sales should be eschewed, since they too often imply an open-ended sales policy. Because of its predominant position as an arms supplier, and because of the relative lack of dependence upon arms exports, the United States is in a unique position to lead the way toward control of the international arms market.

Opportunities for Arms Control

In order to analyze opportunities for constraining the arms trade, a number of questions need to be addressed. Who should be the targets of constraint: the suppliers, the recipients, or both? On what level should efforts at control be concentrated—unilateral, bilateral, regional, or global? What should be controlled—the quantity of weapons, the quality, or the rate of acquisition? Should the constraints be formal or tacit? What should be covered—weapons, ammunition, spare parts, training, licenses? In this section we will deal briefly with only the first two questions.

Although consumer agreements to reduce the demand for arms are more likely to succeed than producer-imposed restrictions, one recent development offers a precedent for producer restraint. A seven-nation group representing the major exporters of nuclear technology has agreed to set standards and regulate exports by its members. According to reports of the agreement, the seven nations—Great Britain, France, West Germany, Canada, Japan, the Soviet Union, and the United States—undertake not to seek competitive commercial advantages by weakening provisions concerning safeguards against the use of exported nuclear technology for the production of nuclear weapons. These provisions would also be extended to retransfers of nuclear imports to third countries. However, no enforcement capabilities exist, and the safeguards referred to are generally regarded as inadequate to prevent diversion of nuclear material for military purposes. The model of this committee demonstrates both the feasibility and the weaknesses of suppliers' agreements.

Unilateral restraint is often scoffed at because there are so many arms suppliers. But unilateral moderation by the United States, which accounts for nearly half the world's total arms transactions, may be a prerequisite for successful bilateral or multilateral efforts. The impetus for unilateral limitations might come from either Congress or the executive branch. Congress, in the vetoed version of the 1976 Arms Export Control Act, proposed a $9 billion worldwide ceiling for United States arms sales. Ceilings are difficult to make operational and often have a tendency to become floors. They do, however, offer the advantage of forcing an ordering of priorities, of setting some means of weighing sales to one country versus sales to another.

The United States could use its considerable influence in international lending institutions such as the International Monetary Fund (IMF) or the International Bank for Reconstruction and Development (IBRD) to restrict financing to Third World countries that spend a disproportionate share of their national budgets on military expenditures. In the past these international organizations have shied away from public statements or stands on politically sensitive topics such as military spending. However, as the burden of indebtedness of non-OPEC developing countries increases, the lending institutions may be-

97

come less hesitant to press for reductions in military spending and those countries most heavily in debt may become more receptive to such exhortations.

Regional approaches to arms trade limitations are generally considered more likely to succeed than unilateral or global attempts. Many observers hoped that the 1974 Latin American effort to limit arms imports, the Declaration of Ayacucho, would set a useful precedent. In practice, however, the agreement has served simply to illustrate the problems of regional arms limitations. The signers of the Ayacucho Declaration—Argentina, Bolivia, Chile, Colombia, Ecuador, Panama, Peru, and Venezuela—all declared that they would not purchase "offensive weapons of a sophisticated nature." Since the declaration, six of the countries decided to extend the limitation to defensive weapons as well as offensive and to consider thinning out border forces, establishing demilitarized zones, and monitoring weapons inventories.

Philip Farley, former deputy director of the U.S. Arms Control and Disarmament Agency (ACDA), has described four factors crucial to successful arms trade limitations agreements: (1) local initiative, (2) a common background of attention to arms control, (3) a community framework and identity, and (4) a conjunction of interests, such as reducing arms expenditures.[45] All these are present for the Ayacucho signatories, yet since the signing of the declaration, all the major countries have purchased supersonic combat aircraft and increased the size of their armed forces. Several nations have accelerated their plans for indigenous arms production.

There are at least four ways the United States unilaterally could cooperate with and encourage the Ayacucho signers:

1. By refraining from promoting arms sales to participant countries and their neighbors
2. By establishing a policy of not responding to arms requests from apostate members of the treaty group

[45] Philip J. Farley, Briefing to Arms Trade Subpanel, United Nations Association Conventional Arms Control Policy Panel, Aspen, Colo., August 1975.

3. By placing the same restrictions on arms exports to all countries in the region, whether or not they are parties to the
agreement

4. By exporting arms only after the signatory nations grant a
regionwide approval for the transaction[46]

Any such unilateral actions by the United States should be
viewed as experiments. Their purpose would be to encourage
reciprocal restraint by other suppliers. If the French or the
Soviets, for example, did not adhere to similar limitations, the
United States would be forced to reconsider its policy.

RECOMMENDATIONS

There are limits to the ability of any one nation to determine the
nature of the arms trade, but the United States can exert greater
influence over the quantity and quality of world arms trade than
any other nation. Three general recommendations for unilateral
action are worth considering.

First, the United States should strongly encourage regional or
national restraint in the purchase of arms. The granting of nonmilitary foreign aid may provide some means of exerting leverage.
For example, the United States could link its level of economic
assistance to the level of national military expenditure of aid
recipients. Any reduction in defense spending would result in
more aid; any increase in defense spending would correspondingly reduce economic assistance. Such a proposal should not
warrant a great deal of optimism. The linkage of foreign aid to
other issues, such as votes in the UN, has generated considerable
resentment in the past and may do so again. Moreover, the
amount of United States foreign economic aid has declined over

[46]These recommendations come from three sources: The Working Group on
Conventional Weapons Control: Latin America, 16th Strategy for Peace Conference, Airlie House, Warrenton, Va., October 1975; "Controlling the International Arms Trade," UNA-USA National Policy Panel on Conventional
Arms Control, April 1976; and Warren Unna, *Foreign Affairs Newsletter*, May
10, 1975.

the past few years; there seems little prospect of an increase substantial enough to permit real diplomatic leverage.

The United States could encourage other nations to restrain their arms trade by providing evidence of its own unilateral restraint. It will have an opportunity to do so in the near future. As new weapons systems are phased into the United States' active inventory, a large number of F-4 fighter aircraft and M-60 tanks will become surplus equipment. There will undoubtedly be a ready market for such equipment, which, even when it is being phased out of the United States' front-line inventory, will still be more sophisticated than the front-line weapons of most nations. By mothballing or even scrapping these weapons rather than transferring them abroad, the United States would check another possibly destabilizing round of regional arms races and perhaps serve as a useful precedent to other producers.

Second, Congress should make the transfer process in future arms transactions more "viscous" by extending the time for debate and discussion within the government and by the public. Congress should have more time to consider proposed arms sales; it should require better justification of sales; it should encourage greater public discussion; and it should make greater use of arms transfer impact statements.

Our third recommendation is that a suppliers' code of conduct for arms exports be established. The code of conduct could be modeled on the nuclear suppliers' agreement, which has established consultative mechanisms on the export of nuclear equipment and technologies. Systems whose primary mission is attack against cities—such as long-range surface-to-surface missiles and area weapons—should be banned from international trade. Second, the distinction between offensive and defensive systems, while highly debatable and filled with ambiguities, could nevertheless serve as another guideline. Systems whose primary mission is offensive, such as strike and interdiction aircraft, self-propelled guns, tanks, and long-range PGMs, should be identified as potentially destabilizing. Their transfer to areas such as the Middle East should be avoided. Third, systems that diminish the likelihood of surprise attack—including elaborate intelligence-gathering and surveillance systems using various types of sensors, electronic monitoring systems, and various types of reconnaissance aircraft—need to be identified; trade in such systems should be encouraged.

Appendix

METHODOLOGICAL PROBLEMS

A number of serious problems face the analyst of international arms trade. The difficulties involve the amount, the comparability, and the soundness of the data available in the public domain. The United States and Sweden both release a substantial amount of information about their own arms transfers, but data from other supplier nations are woefully inadequate. Many recipient nations provide no data at all about their arms acquisitions. In many cases, efforts to secure more information are frustrated by government control of the media.

Even in the United States data gathering is not a simple task. Much of the information concerning arms transactions is classified, usually at the request of the recipient government. In 1975, the first year that the Nelson Amendment was operative, Congress received notification of 45 pending United States arms transactions valued at $25 million or more. Nearly half of these (22) classified all or some of the following information: the prospective purchasing nations, the total estimated value of the item, description of the articles or services rendered. While senators and members of Congress can obtain the classified information if they choose to take the time and effort, it remains unavailable to the American public.

The major publishers of information on worldwide arms transfers are the Stockholm International Peace Research Institute

(SIPRI), the United States Arms Control and Disarmament Agency (ACDA), and the International Institute for Strategic Studies (IISS). There are several problems of comparability of data among governments and even within a single national government. One major difference among various data compilations concerns the definitions of arms transactions. SIPRI lists only "major weapons systems"; such hardware is estimated to cover just about half the dollar value of all military-related transfers. The ACDA includes all weapons, ammunition, and even uniforms in its calculations. The U.S. Defense Department figures include "infrastructure," such as the construction of barracks and roads by the Army Corps of Engineers, under the rubric of military sales. Other nations might consider such assistance to fall more accurately under the heading of general economic aid.

Another problem is the lack of consensus on how to calculate the value of the weapons—whether to express those values in current or constant dollars or in other currencies and how to calculate the exchange rates between various currencies. The prices charged are subject to extreme fluctuations and may not reflect the "value" of the transaction. Weapons may be sold as "loss leaders," that is, at less than actual cost in anticipation that the initial deficits will be recovered by future orders. Or the price to the buyer may be greater than the production cost so that the supplier may recoup some of the research and development investment.

Interest rates vary widely, and repayment schedules may range from a few years to more than a decade. These difficulties are compounded by the practice of exchanging current arms for future commodities (for example, selling Soviet arms for Egyptian cotton or French arms for Saudi Arabian oil).

There is no agreement among the various data compilers on when to count an arms transfer. Some use the date the *order is placed,* some the date the *contract is signed,* others the date the *export license is granted,* some the date the *item is actually delivered,* and a few the date at which the *weapons become operational.* All this is compounded because the same source may use different references within the same publication without notifying the reader of the irregularities.

A final problem confronting the analyst concerns the value or the reliability of the comparative data. Nowhere is one told how interagency or intergovernmental differences are resolved. These methodological difficulties are regrettable, but they are also probably unavoidable. Problems with data make current assessments difficult and future projections that much more formidable.

There are methodological problems inherent in forecasting techniques which complement those plaguing the use of contemporary arms trade data. Three different techniques have been used in our assessment of the arms trading world of the 1980s. Each has its own difficulties.

The method of analogy, of comparing present and future situations with some past episodes, is one that comes most readily to mind. The main problem has to do with historical uniqueness. The implication, ramifications, causes, and consequences of American arms shipments to Egypt in 1976 may be very different from those that occurred 20 years earlier.

Extrapolation from past trends is another method. The obvious danger here is that the wrong trends may have been examined. There is a temptation to extrapolate from measurable and reliable data. The relative availability of certain data is, however, no guarantee of relevance; also, past trends need not necessarily continue.

A third method is to identify factors that are likely to cause major discontinuities with the past and lead to major changes in the future. Where possible, we have attempted to identify the "checkpoints," the indicators of such impending transformations. Whatever the methodology, levels of uncertainty are necessarily high in a world in a dizzying state of flux.

Conventional Arms Transfers and Control: Producer Restraints

Peter M. Dawkins

ONE

Introduction

Arms transfers are not ends in themselves; they are means to ends. They are techniques of statecraft and instruments of economic policy. As a result, a major obstacle to controlling the arms trade is "the attitude held by supplier and recipient states alike that restrictions on their right to supply or receive arms might limit their ability to achieve important national objectives without bringing them compensating advantages."[1] Why aren't there compensating advantages? Doesn't the presence of arms promote or provoke war? Surely the avoidance of war is an obvious "advantage."

Arms transfers can provoke wars, of course, and sometimes have. An abrupt increase in the quantity of arms available or the provision of more sophisticated armaments in an already tense setting may trigger armed conflict. The war in Angola in 1975, for example, can be said to have been precipitated by the importation of Soviet arms and Cuban troops. In other circumstances, however, in which the existing military situation is unbalanced and one country is threatening to attack a weaker foe, introducing additional arms can steady the situation and make the outbreak of hostilities less likely. Arms transfers can also help stop a war in progress. The measured provision by the United States of weapons and ammunition to Israel during the 1973 Yom Kippur

[1]*The International Transfer of Conventional Arms,* a Report to the Congress from the U.S. Arms Control and Disarmament Agency, April 12, 1974, p. xvii.

War, in response to early Israeli battle losses and Soviet supplies to Egypt, helped turn the tide of the war and bring about a cease-fire.

Because of the contrasting consequences of different arms transfers, no consensus exists regarding what threat, if any, is posed by the spread of conventional arms. Many observers take refuge in the proposition that arms transfers are inherently neither stabilizing nor destabilizing, that the supply of arms is incidental and not a fundamental cause of warfare. The time is now upon us, or soon will be, however, when that attitude will require revision. The past 15 years have seen the value of conventional arms transfers increase by a factor of 4; orders for arms have increased even more dramatically. The type of military material being transferred has changed from outdated, surplus equipment to brand new, major weapons systems, sometimes not yet in the operational inventory of the producing country's armed forces.

Arms transfers of this sort and magnitude have consequences of their own, distinct from the objectives being sought by those who supply them. Small-scale armed forces of developing countries, when provided with a few additional items of obsolescent equipment, tend not to become dominant factors in themselves. But when billions of dollars in up-to-date, sophisticated weapons accumulate in a region, their presence develops a momentum of its own, and the vastly increased military capability by itself constitutes a new and important dynamic. For one thing, large-scale arms transfers make possible the creation of regional hegemones, although in any given instance (that of Iran, for example) assuring its hegemony may have been incidental to the objectives that motivated producer countries to provide those arms. As a result, these and other consequences—intended and unintended—must be considered, along with the more basic objectives being sought, in any judgment of the wisdom of arms transfers.

Nonetheless, this essay does not proceed from the assumption that arms transfers are inherently undesirable. However, it does assume that there is no "invisible hand" guaranteeing that any pattern of transfers, left unchecked, will automatically be helpful or wise. Furthermore, it is recognized that, from a practical standpoint, nonarmament can be achieved much more readily than disarmament. Therefore, to the extent that uncertainties and disagreements exist regarding the wisdom of increasing the level of armaments in an area, it would seem preferable to limit their growth in the first place rather than confront the need later to reduce levels already established.

There may seem to be a certain patronizing tone in this discussion, deriving almost unavoidably from the fact that the perspective is that of "producer" restraint. If those states with the ability to purchase or the inclination to petition for arms they cannot produce were unfailingly wise, or if the consequences of their acquiring arms were limited exclusively to their countries alone, the issue of producer restraint would be of only peripheral interest. However, in reality the effects are often global and the consequences potentially catastrophic. Moreover, producers are hardly "passive" elements in the complex chemistry of arms transfers. The billions of dollars in profits and the crucial political objectives sought through the provision of arms surely prompt producer governments to stimulate arms appetites among potential customers in certain circumstances. Consequently, a pure laissez faire approach can hardly be depended upon to advance the goal of a moderate world order; the alternative, seeking to control the international flow of arms from the producer side of the equation, deserves careful consideration.

Not all categories of conventional arms transfers can feasibly be controlled. Small arms and ammunition exist in such abundance throughout the world, and can be manufactured so easily and cheaply in so many countries, that it is impossible to imagine an arrangement by which their transfer could be realistically controlled from the producer side. Although the sources of supply for artillery pieces, most conventional munitions, and military wheeled vehicles are somewhat more limited, it seems similarly vain to suppose that they could be effectively restricted either. At the other end of the spectrum of sophistication, there are certain ultracomplex systems, such as nuclear submarines and aircraft carriers, for which the demand and sources of supply are inherently restricted.

Between the two extremes is a realm that includes armored vehicles, all but the most sophisticated combat aircraft, current generations of precision-guided munitions, naval patrol craft, and destroyers. With the predictable diffusion of technological skills, this middle realm will, toward the end of the 1980s, also include such currently ultracomplex wonders as electro-optics, laser-guidance systems, and many other new electronic battlefield systems. These are the armaments fields in which the required technical sophistication is substantial but still achievable by a variety of producer countries; the price is high but affordable for many of the prospective recipients; and the military advantage gained from incorporating the armaments into one's armed forces—especially if potential opponents do not possess similar weaponry or, more urgently, if they already do—is sufficient to motivate selected countries to acquire them. It is on this middle realm of weapons technology that those who would seek to control arms transfers from the producer side would profit most by focusing their attention.

Given this perspective, the analysis that follows examines the pattern of incentives motivating producers to export arms as well as those counterincentives that might be stimulated to disincline them from doing so. On the presumption that there are some circumstances in which it would be desirable to restrict arms transfers, Chapter 3 outlines a series of steps that, if taken together, could provide a degree of control. The approach described in that chapter is geared toward "achievability." It does not call for a dramatic rearrangement of the international order, nor does it require any abrupt changes in individual countries' behavior. What it does do is capitalize on the opportunities for collaboration among producer countries that already exist today and those that can reasonably be expected to emerge in the 1980s. Since this is admittedly only a partial prescription, Chapter 4 describes what lies beyond it and the additional ingredients needed to establish a more comprehensive and systematic program of control.

In all of this, one major artificial distinction is drawn. The analysis addresses only the producer side of the arms transfers phenomenon, when in fact the prospects for control would seem to be best advanced through the efforts of producers and recipients working together. Although not discussed in this essay, their interaction will play an important role in determining what path is ultimately followed in the years ahead.

112

TWO

The Producer Community

DESCRIPTION

To the extent that knives and clubs are weapons, all countries are weapons producers, and always have been. Even narrowing the category somewhat, limiting it to explosively projected munitions and related systems, a large number of countries still qualify as producers—most of whom manufacture a portion of the small arms and ammunition used domestically. The field rapidly diminishes, however, when the definition is confined to those countries that produce militarily significant armaments, and it shrinks further still when limited to those who export such weapons. Even so, there were 50 countries whose arms exports exceeded a million dollars between 1965 and 1974.[2] The U.S. Arms Control and Disarmament Agency (ACDA) classifies nine countries as "major suppliers," and of those, the combined exports of the United States and the Soviet Union accounted for 78 percent of the world total during the decade 1965–1974. When the exports of the major European producers and Canada are added, 93 percent of the total is accounted for.[3] Table 1 lists the export totals for the nine major suppliers in 1974 and over the 10-year period from 1965 to 1974.

[2] *World Military Expenditures and Arms Transfers, 1965–1974,* U.S. Arms Control and Disarmament Agency, Washington, D.C., 1975, Table IV, pp. 56–72.
[3] Ibid.

The grouping of producers in Table 1 underscores the basic structure of the producer community. While it is valid to treat the Soviet–East European segment as a bloc, the North Atlantic cluster is today more a geographic locus than a tightly integrated unit. To the major countries listed, four additional producers must be added which, though considerably smaller, nonetheless combine to add another increment to the total of conventional arms exports: Sweden ($37 million), Belgium ($36 million), Norway ($27 million), and Switzerland ($23 million).[4] Substantial differences of policy regarding arms transfers exist among the countries of the North Atlantic group. Sweden and West Germany, on the one hand, have consistently refused to provide arms

TABLE 1
Arms Transfers: Value*

	1965–1974 Totals, Millions (current dollars)		1974 Totals, Millions (current dollars)	
North Atlantic				
United States	31,563	(49.0%)	4,160	(45.2%)
France	2,826	(4.4)	561	(.6.0)
United Kingdom	2,089	(3.2)	463	(5.0)
Federal Republic of Germany	1,221	(1.9)	223	(2.4)
Canada	1,187	(1.8)	109	(1.2)
	38,886	(60.3%)	5,516	(59.8%)
Soviet/Eastern European				
Soviet Union	18,793	(29.2%)	2,810	(30.4%)
Czechoslovakia	1,253	(1.9)	76	(0.8)
Poland	1,228	(1.9)	20	(0.2)
	21,274	(33.0%)	2,906	(31.4%)

[4]Ibid. (1974 export figure is in current dollars.)

114

TABLE 1 (continued)
Arms Transfers: Value*

	1965–1974 Totals, Millions (current dollars)	1974 Totals, Millions (current dollars)
China	2,119 (3.3%)	322 (3.5%)
All others	2,125 (3.3%)	486 (5.3%)
World Total	64,404	9,230

**Definition of Arms Transfers:* Arms transfers represent the international transfer under grant, credit, cash, of commercial sales terms of military equipment usually referred to as "conventional," including weapons of war, parts thereof, ammunition, support equipment, and other commodities considered primarily military in nature. . . . Excluded by definition are nuclear, chemical, and biological weapons, and strategic missile systems. Also excluded are foodstuffs, medical equipment, and other items potentially useful to the military but with alternative civilian uses. Training and technical services are not included. The statistics published here are estimates of the value of goods actually delivered during the reference year, in contrast to the value of programs, agreements, contracts, or orders which may result in a future transfer of goods.

SOURCE: *World Military Expenditures and Arms Transfers, 1965–1974,* U.S. Arms Control and Disarmament Agency, Washington, D.C., 1975, Table IV, pp. 56–72, and Table V, p. 73.

to areas of conflict, while France, on the other hand, has aggressively marketed its military wares wherever customers could be found. In addition, the burgeoning Middle East arms trade (comprising 70 percent of total world orders placed for armaments over the past three years) has witnessed intense and sometimes bitter competition among the North Atlantic suppliers. Saudi Arabia provides two immediate illustrations of this competition. One is the continuing contest between the United States and France for the supply of fighter aircraft (F-5 versus Mirage) and main battle tanks (M-60 versus AMX-30). Another example is the fierce competition between the United States and Great Britain over who will provide the communications needed to integrate the Saudi air defense systems. Saudi Arabia currently operates both American and British interceptor aircraft as well as American Hawk anti-aircraft missiles; building the communications network to link these separate elements into a coordinated system means a billion dollar contract.

Projecting ahead into the 1980s, three major developments are likely to occur in the producer community:

1. The increased "commercialization" of arms transfers
2. The emergence of China and Japan as major producers
3. The proliferation of "second-tier" producers and the growth of co-producers

With regard to "commercialization," the post-World War II evolution of arms transfers from grant aid through sales financed with long-term, low-rate loans to commercial cash and credit sales is likely to continue. Increasingly, the governments of industrialized nations will be squeezed between the two jaws— one domestic and one international—of an economic pincer. Domestically, the demand in all societies, authoritarian and democratic alike, for improved medical treatment, education, housing, care for the aged, and other services will put pressure on governments to lower defense costs in order to free the extra budget dollars required to finance these enlarged social programs. Selling military arms and equipment abroad will be seen as one way to escape this pressure, since the resulting higher production will lower unit prices and reduce the procurement costs for indigenous armed forces. Internationally, the rising price of natural resources will exert continuing pressure on importing industrialized countries to increase their export earnings in order to maintain a tolerable balance-of-payments position. Even though they are not one of the major export accounts, arms sales do contribute positively in this regard.

The growth of co-production and retransfers will alter the patterns of demand for arms. Moreover, as the costs and difficulty of maintaining high-complexity weapons systems become excessive, demand may shift back to less sophisticated although still modern equipment. But this altered pattern of demand will not be accompanied by a return to earlier patterns of transaction; the economic pressures on industrialized producer states will persist, and consequently their early pattern of largesse—giving away, or selling cheaply, surplus equipment—characteristic of the first two post-World War II decades, will not reemerge. Instead commercial transactions will remain the rule.

The second development one can expect in the producer community during the 1980s is the emergence of two new major producers: China and Japan. The ACDA catalog already labels China a "major producer," and it is true that Chinese arms exports far surpass those of the Eastern European countries and are comparable in total value to those of the larger Western European producers. It is difficult to predict any future development with respect to China, and assessing its future motivation as an arms supplier is no exception. In the past, China has provided arms and equipment to neighboring countries, both communist and noncommunist. Support for North Vietnam during the war there (and for North Korea in 1951–1953) was both a demonstration of solidarity with a "fraternal anti-imperialist" state and a counter to Soviet efforts to gain power and influence in the area. Similarly, Chinese willingness to provide arms to Pakistan can be explained as a step designed to develop regional political leverage and to counter Soviet military support of India. This sort of action will undoubtedly continue. Outside Asia, China has generally been very circumspect with regard to arms transfers, apparently preferring, at least for the time being, to employ other forms of aid and assistance.[5] As the stakes grow and opportunities present

[5]Chinese military support for the anti-Soviet factions in the Angolan civil war was quite limited, and was rapidly curtailed as Soviet involvement increased. Evidently Peking was reluctant to get too deeply involved in a conflict so far from its own shores. Most Chinese aid to Southern Africa and elsewhere has thus far been economic.

themselves in Africa and the Pacific, however, post-Mao China may well become more assertive and willing to export arms in order to further its national objectives. In addition, internal development needs in the 1980s will lead to an expansion of China's international trade, and this will create increasing requirements for convertible currencies. In response it is quite possible that the Chinese will turn to arms sales as one source.

In candor, however, it must be admitted that the magnitude of Chinese arms exports cannot be confidently predicted. Much depends on how extensive China's oil production proves to be, and on its ability to generate hard-currency requirements by means of oil sales. For any of a number of reasons—reduced competition with the Soviet Union, ideological moderation, or a greater domestic orientation on the part of the post-Mao leadership—Chinese interest in supporting revolutionary movements could diminish, thereby lessening the motivation for arms transfers. Furthermore, whatever movements are supported are likely not to have superpower enemies (like the United States in Southeast Asia), necessitating massive arsenals. Nonetheless, the Chinese are capable of producing the entire spectrum of modern tanks, artillery, missiles, and munitions, and the prospect of their presenting a significant presence on the arms transfer landscape of the future cannot be ignored.

Japan has the technological and industrial capability to become a major contender in the field of arms transfers. The economic advantages to be gained from arms exports may well overcome the legacy of antimilitarism that has restrained Japanese policy heretofore. Even though export earnings from arms sales would be small in comparison with total export earnings, the pressure of higher petroleum prices is profound. Japan already produces aircraft and tanks, and the temptation to reduce unit costs through larger-scale production could lead to a major role for Tokyo in the international arms business. One possibility is that Japan will provide to second-tier producers those sophisticated subsystems—such as advanced electronics, electro-optics, special metals, and precision casting—that depend on high technologies.

The proliferation and growth of these second-tier producers is the third development that seems highly probable in the 1980s. Countries such as Spain, Italy, Yugoslavia, Australia, and Israel are representative of the second tier. These producers deserve special attention because they are or are becoming highly industrialized and will clearly have the capability to produce systems of moderate technological sophistication during the next 10 years. In addition, in many cases they are countries not so closely tied to the United States or the Soviet Union that they will be responsive to or constrained by the policy leads of the superpowers. As a result, the situation may well develop that prospective arms recipients will have access to an expanding range of free-lance suppliers, fully capable of producing much of what the recipients desire.

One group of second-tier countries will be those that become producers by virtue of co-production agreements concluded with major producers. Co-production—the collaboration between an experienced producer and a would-be producer in the construction and operation of a new arms industry in the latter's country—is not new, of course. It has frequently been an element of United States–European agreements on joint production of weapons systems for NATO, and undoubtedly will become increasingly prominent in future agreements aimed at standardization in the design and specialization in the manufacture of military equipment in the North Atlantic community. Since all the parties involved are already established producers in their own right and share a heritage of long-standing political linkages, co-production in the NATO context does not constitute a dramatic new development within the producer community. By contrast, co-production arrangements with countries, such as Taiwan, not previously capable of domestic arms production are potentially much farther reaching. Two consequences are particularly important. First, the growth of indigenous production resulting from co-production reduces to some degree the dependence of former recipient states upon industrialized nations for their supply of military arms and equipment. Second, producer states, by assisting certain developing countries to become arms producers, may unavoidably contribute to their becoming arms exporters too. A particular concern is that these derivative producer states may adopt arms transfer policies contrary to those of the traditional producers, thereby obstructing the achievement of whatever political or strategic objectives may be at stake. Iran is an example of a country that, were it to become a major independent arms exporter in the Middle East, could conceivably pursue regional hegemony in a manner obstructive of American or European purposes. The magnitude of this threat is limited, however, since the likely extent of residual dependency (in the case of Iran, specifically, but for other second-tier producers and co-producers as well), in the form of industrial technologies not yet developed, suggests that these states' freedom of action will remain circumscribed. Nonetheless, the emergence of additional producers with a certain degree of independence and potentially different political perspectives could significantly complicate the problem of controlling arms transfers.

INCENTIVES FOR ARMS TRANSFERS: MOTIVATING FACTORS AND HOW THEY INFLUENCE DIFFERENT PRODUCERS

Producers provide arms to nonproducers because they deem it useful to do so. Charity and chance do not motivate them; conscious calculation of self-interest does. A particular arms transfer may be a mistake, but it is not an accident. Many identifiable influences affect the decisions of producer-country governments or industries to enter into arms transfers deals. While each case is unique, evaluating the prospects for controlling arms transfers in the future requires, first, a systematic cataloging of these influences.

Four categories of factors—economic, strategic, political-diplomatic, and ideological—are described below. The major incentives for arms producers to provide weapons to others are included in those categories. In addition, there are certain psychological and cultural influences, principally those deriving from notions of sovereignty and grandeur, that also affect the propensity of producer states to transfer arms. Although they operate through mechanisms included in one or more of the four listed categories, the subtle but pervasive influence of these psychological and cultural factors deserves highlighting at the outset.

The capacity to defend oneself against armed attack is the irreducible minimum of sovereignty. The checkered history of treaties and alliances has led national leaders to conclude that the ideal circumstance is one in which they are dependent upon no one but themselves to guarantee their essential defense. Achieving this independence has come to be seen as requiring not only a competent force in readiness, but also a domestic industrial capacity to sustain that force in combat. Realistically, only the superpowers can approach such a condition; minor powers do not even try. In between, the major European producers—France, England, and Germany—although unable to achieve complete military and industrial self-reliance, have persevered in the conviction that maintaining a broadly based domestic defense industry is a prudent hedge against potentially crippling isolation. Since their own armed forces do not have continuing requirements sufficient to absorb the output of major armaments industries, they must turn to foreign sales in order to preserve this dimension of national sovereignty.

Military forces and equipment are more than a means of defense and conquest, of course; they are also symbols of national competence and prowess, elements of a complex and elusive property called "national grandeur." Like nationalism, grandeur combines pride and a sense of history and rests, to a substantial extent, upon others' acceptance that one is self-assertive, powerful, and in the forefront of scientific and technological progress. France under de Gaulle provides unquestionably the most dramatic twentieth-century example of a quest for national grandeur. France's construction of its own nuclear-tipped ballistic missiles, the so-called *Force de Frappe*, was the most extreme aspect (and these were not transferred to other countries' forces); but the presence of Mirage aircraft in air forces on various continents is unquestionably viewed by French officials as a litmus of the continuing legitimacy of France's claim to a prominent place in

121

the world. In somewhat more moderate and less conscious ways, this need to bolster the national ego is one of the factors motivating many other producer states to transfer arms. In pursuit of national grandeur, regional powers such as Brazil and Iran with great power ambitions might in the future seek to become arms exporters as a way of impressing the rest of the world.

Economic Factors

In the early post-World War II period, when arms transfers consisted mainly of surplus equipment provided in the form of grants, economic incentives were of minor importance. Since that time, however, with the increase in cost of weaponry, the growth of global economic interdependence, and the commercialization of arms trade, economic considerations have become major factors. The fivefold increase in the price of OPEC oil, resulting in petrodollar affluence for the oil-producing nations and monetary outflows for most of the industrialized world, has added another economic element to the full array of factors prompting arms sales.

For the United States, increased oil prices have created an annual drain of $20 billion on the *balance of payments*, only partially offset by OPEC countries' investments in the United States. Less than two months after the oil embargo was announced, President Nixon created an interagency task force to examine all feasible ways of stimulating exports, specifically citing arms sales as a prime potential candidate. The increased cost of raw materials—particularly but not only of petroleum—faces all industrialized countries with the major problem of maintaining a favorable balance of payments. The export of military hardware, support systems, and support services is an attractive solution because it involves sizable amounts of money (up to 15 percent of total exports in some cases), and because the commodities and services involved are high-value-added items (that is, they generate a high per-unit level of income relative to other exports). Even for countries such as Great Britain, France, Sweden, and Switzerland, for whom arms transfers constitute only a small percentage of total exports, when the balance of payments is only slightly out of equilibrium, foreign military sales can make the difference between a surplus and a deficit.

The Arab oil boycott and the emergence of the "oil weapon" brought into clear view another economic factor, the *fear of being deprived of resources*. The industrialized countries, with the exception of the Soviet Union, have demands for raw materials that cannot be met by domestic sources. A desire to secure guaranteed access to foreign sources of those materials essential to the functioning of their national economies has for many years encouraged certain producer countries to export arms; arms sales have long been seen as a way to buy the friendship of raw-material-exporting states. The post-World War II pattern of arms transfers from the United Kingdom to certain Commonwealth trading partners, as an example, suggests that it was motivated in part by the desire to maintain the flow of raw materials to Great Britain. On the other hand, the more resource-independent United States perceived itself until October 1973 as essentially insulated against any pressures of limited resource supply; but the oil embargo precipitously shattered this perception, and the subsequent dramatic increase in United States arms deliveries to and orders for United States equipment by Middle East oil countries can be seen as Washington's attempt to deter future embargos or severe cutbacks.

More than as a means of buying friendship and of offsetting oil-derived balance-of-payments deficits, many oil-consuming arms producers undoubtedly see arms transfers as a way of expanding economic relations with oil-producing states. Doing so creates bonds of economic interdependence that the arms recipients might not be willing to jeopardize with another oil embargo. It is unclear whether cartel action similar to that in oil can or will occur in other resource fields. Nonetheless, the growth in arms transfers to other primary commodity-exporting countries in recent years indicates that the rationale, the desire to avert resource deprivation, is operating in the minds of arms-producing states.

Another economic factor of growing importance is the problem of *unit cost*. Research and development costs, particularly for weapon systems of middle and high sophistication, are increasing

123

at an almost runaway rate. Since R&D costs are customarily amortized over the full production run, the unit price a producer country must pay for its own inventory of such equipment is a function of the total number of items produced. Obviously, if substantial numbers can be sold abroad, the cost to the armed forces of the producer country is correspondingly reduced. In addition, the competitive position on the international market of a particular piece of equipment improves as its unit cost declines. The intense competition among the United States, France, and Sweden to be selected by the four-nation European consortium as the choice for supplying the replacement for the F-104 provides a recent vivid illustration of the power of this incentive.

It is also the case that modern, complex, sophisticated production lines simply cannot be switched on and off at will. As a result, there is an obvious benefit to keeping production lines "hot," that is, avoiding slack periods in production schedules during which fixed costs drive up the average cost per unit of output. Larger production runs made possible by export sales provide a means of smoothing out production schedules for increased efficiency and profitability.

A related factor of special significance for producers other than the major powers is that of *minimum economic size*. A number of producer countries' armed forces are not large enough to generate sufficient orders for military hardware or make it economically feasible to possess an arms industry (or at least particular arms industries) at all. Yet, as noted earlier, an arms-production capacity may be desired as an assurance of national sovereignty, or as a demonstration of international stature. The best way to support such industries is to sell sufficient quantities of arms on the international market to achieve the necessary minimum economic size. The French combat aircraft and British tank industries have been sustained on this basis for more than a decade.

Employment is another economic consideration that encourages producer countries to export arms. Arms exports and the related support and training activity mean jobs. Some observers estimate that for every $1 billion in goods and services that the United States exports, $2 billion is added to the United States

GNP, and 40,000 to 70,000 jobs are created. At a time when industrialized countries in the West are experiencing disturbingly high levels of unemployment, all sources of jobs are precious. As foreign arms sales increase employment levels and keep firms and corporations alive, those sales are encouraged and aggressively pursued. The fact that, in economic terms, increasing nonmilitary production for domestic markets would theoretically bring about an even greater rise in employment and GNP does not negate this appeal, since transferring resources from existing arms production for export into industrial production for domestic consumption would involve both uncertainty and major market dislocations.

Indeed, the issue of dislocations makes the employment incentive even greater than is suggested by the magnitude of the economic benefits involved. In most countries, the number of people employed in arms industries is small compared to the total size of the national work force. Nonetheless, as in many industries, employment tends to be concentrated in specific locales and in particular manufacturing fields. As a result, the fear of dislocation and economic hardship attendant to any anticipated reduction in arms production is translated into potent political currency. Proposals to reduce foreign arms sales are met, therefore, by sharp political opposition.

Although its importance has been diminished to a certain extent by the evolution from the "mobilization" mentality of the 1930s and 1940s to a strategy of "forces in readiness" today, the capability for *industrial mobilization* in wartime nonetheless remains in many leaders' minds the bedrock of national defense. Since the demand for armaments tends to follow an irregular cycle, it is judged desirable to retain the potential to revitalize arms production on a major scale even during periods in the cycle when the immediate equipment needs of a country's armed forces are marginal or nil. Since the lead time required to reconstitute heavy defense industries from scratch is too long for mobilization purposes, there is strong incentive to maintain a "warm" production base as insurance in the event major new production may be required on short notice to meet the needs of national armed forces.[6] The most feasible way to do so is to market sufficient arms abroad to keep the production facilities in operation.

Strategic Factors

For the superpowers, the objectives most frequently sought through arms transfers over the past 30 years have been strategic ones. In the 10 years following World War II, the United States and the Soviet Union were the only significant arms suppliers, and each of them provided military equipment for the same avowed reason: to promote collective security. The Soviets supplied their allies in Eastern Europe, China, and North Korea, while the United States supplied the countries of NATO, the Central Treaty Organization (CENTO), and SEATO, plus South Korea and Taiwan.

That rationale continued through the 1960s, with massive quantities of arms being provided to both sides in the Vietnam War, especially as the actual American presence was phased out pursuant to the "Nixon Doctrine." At the same time, other nations joined the producer ranks, with many of the NATO countries and to a lesser extent certain of the Warsaw Pact members (specifically Czechoslovakia and Poland) becoming arms exporters.

Today, the strategic objectives sought through arms transfers extend beyond collective security to such vital strategic issues as basing, access, and overflight rights. With France and England no longer global powers, these objectives are in most respects the province of the United States and the Soviet Union—although to a certain extent, France's aggressiveness in arms exports is a reflection of her desire to exert an independent though secondary

[6]The experience of the United States in 1973 provides a dramatic illustration of the mechanism involved. The U.S. Army's demand for new tanks had diminished during the early 1970s to the point that only one turret and hull casting foundry remained in operation. Other previously used foundries were sold and dismantled. Following the October 1973 Arab-Israeli War, there suddenly developed a demand for dramatically increased levels of tank production. It took the United States more than a year (and a great deal of extra money) to reequip and reconstitute the old foundries so that production could be increased to the rates desired.

influence in a world of more than two dimensions. For their part, the superpowers seek to gain a broader and more substantial basis from which to project their military power worldwide. Most recently the Soviets have employed arms "persuasion" in Somalia, using military aid to acquire naval base rights and, in a more interventionist manner via the Cubans, in Angola. Earlier arms assistance by the United States to Turkey, Greece, and Thailand provided important access to those areas; uncertainty regarding the future availability of base and access rights is a source of serious concern to American security planners.

Political-Diplomatic Factors

The political-diplomatic motives for selling arms arise from the desire to win friends whose resultant military strength is, at best, of secondary interest. For example, in supplying arms to Peru, the Soviets have less interest in Peruvian military strength or the prospects for Soviet base rights than they do in creating political bonds with a country in the heart of the Western Hemisphere. Proxies can exert political leverage in addition to, or instead of, acting as military surrogates; the provision of conventional military equipment and training have been the standard way for arms producers to secure political influence and cement proxy relationships. Overall, the key to operating effectively in the complex domain of the international system is the possession of political allies to intercede on one's behalf, to help persuade third parties to adopt favorable positions, and to provide support in the UN and other world organizations as well as in regional groupings and forums. Many means are employed to foster these relationships and forge a sense of shared interest; the provision of arms and related support equipment has proven to be particularly effective in this regard. Indications are that, throughout the 1980s, the practice will continue to be viewed by the governments of most of the producer states as politically advantageous.

Not only are arms transfers intended to achieve diplomatic and political influence, they also have a habit of engendering an important political flux of their own. For example, the political controversies among NATO members surrounding arms produc-

127

tion for the alliance have sometimes overshadowed the strategic purpose of collective defense. Indeed, the sensitivity of Western European governments to what they regard as American unwillingness to accept anything less than full autonomy in the production of major weapons systems has been a persistent and difficult political hurdle for the alliance.

Ideological Factors

Soviet foreign policy proclaims the legitimacy of support for wars of national liberation on the grounds that the remaining remnants of corrupt colonial regimes can only be transformed by violent overthrow. As a result, dissident groups and radical governments expressing revolutionary goals and espousing Marxist-Leninist doctrine can expect Soviet assistance, often in the form of military arms and equipment. United States foreign policy ostensibly aims at promoting nation-building, based on the belief that disorder and instability undermine a people's well-being, destroy chances for economic progress, and lead to radical tyranny. This policy, like that of the Soviets, often leads to arms transfers, although in the case of the United States the arms are provided solely to ruling authorities in order to help them maintain essential order and stability.

In most cases, ideological reasons for supplying arms overlap with, and are cited to legitimize, strategic, political, and economic concerns. Soviet military support for Angola can be seen as an attempt not only to establish a Marxist-oriented regime but also to secure a foothold for Soviet political and strategic influence in southern Africa. United States arms transfers to certain Third World countries aimed at supporting regimes threatened by radical opposition are often also motivated by a desire to protect American business interests and to maintain political leverage in the region.

INCENTIVES AND COUNTERINCENTIVES: PROSPECTS FOR THE 1980s

From the preceding analysis of the factors that motivate producer states to transfer arms, certain patterns emerge. The discussion now turns to likely developments in each of the four categories during the 1980s, and to an assessment of how these developments may influence the inclination of producer states to promote arms transfers.

Economic Factors

As discussed above, the conviction that sovereignty and national survival depend upon, or are best advanced by, the possession of a self-contained domestic arms industry exerts a substantial though sometimes subconscious influence on the propensity of industrial countries to export arms. Because of the necessity that an arms industry be of "minimum economic size" and maintain a "warm production base," the desire to avoid dependence on someone else's industrial capacity encourages producer countries to stimulate sales and compete energetically in the international arms market.

But is this conviction well founded? Does it reflect accurately the factors at work today and likely to develop in the 1980s? It is clearer and clearer that this viewpoint is an anachronism, one that ignores profound developments of the past decade. Military thinkers in the United States and in Europe have come to agree that the likelihood of a modern-day replay of World War II in Europe is extremely small. This realization was consummated by the example of the 1973 Arab-Israeli War, in which the extremely high lethality of the modern battlefield was unequivocally displayed. The fact that in 20 days, more tanks were lost than the United States then possessed in its entire European inventory finally buried the assumption that a major NATO–Warsaw Pact war would last long enough to permit mobilizing the arsenals of democracy. It is now appreciated that such a conflict would be a "come-as-you-are" affair, rapidly fought to whatever outcome—stalemate, conclusive resolution, or nuclear escalation—with the military arms and equipment already in existence at the time the war erupted.

If this concept is valid, then maintaining a domestic production-mobilization capacity—as opposed to the capacity to sustain resupply out of standing stocks—is no longer terribly relevant to the outcome of a major war in Europe. Everyone simply does not have to be able to produce cannons and tanks and aircraft, or even aspire to do so. Individual countries of Western Europe may choose to have "complete" arms industries, but it can be cogently argued that reasonable prudence and regard for national sovereignty no longer demand it.

There are important implications in this for the future of "standardization" within NATO and for the possibility of establishing some form of division of labor among North Atlantic arms producers. Both these goals may be more easily achievable if all countries realize how unimportant it is for each to be able to manufacture all types of weapons independently. Standardization could, in turn, have important implications for the future of worldwide arms transfers, since the practice of selling arms to the rest of the world to maintain a potential for mobilization would no longer be essential.

A potentially far-reaching counterincentive to the expansion of arms transfers stems from the increasing frequency of co-production agreements and technology transfers that accompany many present arms transactions. At present, self-restraint on the part of any one supplier is often quixotic, being "rewarded" simply by another supplier stepping in. Nowhere is this phenomenon more apparent than in co-production and technology-transfer agreements. Increasingly, recipient states demand, as a condition of arms sales agreements, that specified production facilities be constructed and full indigenous management and production teams be trained. This demand confronts producers with a dilemma: in the short term, establishing production facilities and training the technical work force to manufacture sophisticated armaments means jobs, income, and balance-of-payments receipts for the producer country. Over the longer term, however, as the client state's production expands, it satisfies indigenously at least a portion of the demand previously supplied by the traditional producer. It is even possible that these co-producers will come to compete in outside markets as well. Producer-country governments, concerned with the continuing economic consequences of their arms transfers policies, undoubtedly recognize this long-term economic danger and are inclined to be cautious. The problem is complicated, though, by the fact that if one country refuses to participate in a co-production arrangement, another seems ready to step in to do so. Under such circumstances, refusing to meet the co-production demands of recipients could leave the individual producer as both the short- and the long-term economic loser.

Throughout the past 30 years, economic factors have had a more forceful impact on the United States and the countries of Western Europe than on the Soviet Union and Eastern European arms suppliers. Should Japan become a significant supplier of armaments, such a move would undoubtedly be prompted largely by economic imperatives. In all probability, the economic considerations discussed above will continue to exert a major influence on the arms transfer policies of the Western producers throughout the 1980s.

It is much more difficult to predict just what impact economic factors will have on Soviet and East European producers in the next decade. The Soviets are not so affluent that they can be cavalier about the cost of their arms transfers. Yet historically they have provided arms on generous terms, either in the form of grants or at reduced prices through low-interest loans repayable in local currency over a 10- to 12-year period. Despite the fact that they have recently begun to require repayment in hard currencies, economic motivation remains today a secondary consideration in Soviet arms transfers policy. A look at the principal recipients of Soviet arms shows that strategic, political, and ideological concerns remain paramount. While economics undoubtedly will become relatively more important to them in the decade ahead as they seek to acquire more and more expensive Western technology—and their hard-currency problems will unquestionably persist—it is unlikely that economic considerations will come to exert as prominent an influence on Soviet and Eastern European arms producers as on those of the West. This situation will be the result of the relatively closed nature of their economies, their far lesser degree of dependence on imported raw materials, an internal market large enough to sustain large-scale, low-unit-cost arms industries without exports, and the absence of domestic unemployment as an incentive for expanding weapons production. Indeed, the difference in commercial emphasis between the producers from the North Atlantic group and those from the Soviet bloc provides the basis for one of the policy prescriptions developed in Chapter 3.

Strategic Factors

One of the previously described incentives for arms transfers is their usefulness in gaining operating, basing, access, and over-flight rights in areas of geographic importance. While arms transfers clearly can and do serve this purpose, it is also the case that the resultant access is anything but permanent and guaranteed. One has only to reflect upon the recent experience of the United States in Turkey and Thailand or of the Soviets in Egypt to appreciate the lack of dependability and assurance in such arrangements. However, many of the agreements that are currently in force do depend on arms transfer provisions. While the arms aspect is ordinarily only one of the variables in the equation causing one country to grant base rights to another, it is often the "sweetener" that makes the agreement viable. The arms provisions may be explicitly written into the formal agreement itself, or they may exist in a tacit agreement to give arms as a portion of the sum paid for the base rights. Because of the importance of these arms provisions to the recipients, and in the absence of any practical alternative, the "unreliability" of certain recipients is unlikely to diminish the willingness of producer countries to sell arms in return for the geographic basis essential to projecting military power abroad.

On the other hand, the time has come when responsible leaders are increasingly aware of and concerned about the consequences deriving from arms transfers. Global security relationships are becoming increasingly loose: an arms producer's sale of weapons for the purpose of maintaining East-West balance may be sought by the recipient with different ends in mind—including local aggression, influence, or coercion. Both the United States and the Soviet Union share a strong desire not to aggravate regional antagonisms in such a way that they might escalate into warfare between the superpowers. The situation is especially delicate in the Arab-Israeli, Indian-Pakistani, and North Korean–South Korean circumstances where one partner is closely associated with the United States and the other with the Soviet Union. Even in instances in which the danger of great-power confrontation is slight, there is the risk that providing sophisticated arms to local military forces could create very potent future adversaries for the great powers themselves.

Neither the unreliability of recipients nor the volatility of conflict-ridden regions holds much prospect of reversing the behavior of producer countries in supplying arms in the future. What these factors do, however, is increase the complexity of the issue. Not only must producer countries evaluate the importance and likelihood of achieving the direct foreign policy objectives sought through arms transfers, they must also judge the acceptability of the derivative consequences flowing from the transfers themselves.

In addition to the already mentioned economic consequences of co-production agreements, there are several derivative strategic consequences as well. Specifically, there are two major strategic liabilities associated with such agreements. First, by enabling countries that could not do so on their own to develop a productive capacity for weaponry of moderate sophistication, producer countries lose control over the eventual disposition of the materiel. Very complex, high-technology systems, such as submarines and high-performance aircraft, probably require too extensive an industrial and technological infrastructure for Brazil, Pakistan, Korea, or other medium powers to develop in the foreseeable future, even with outside assistance. But in the field of precision-guided munitions (which are sophisticated but do not require "heavy" industrial capacity), co-production is already under way and likely to expand. Contracts for co-production of American Maverick and tube-launched, optically tracked, wire-guided (TOW) missiles were recently concluded between the United States and Iran. Since these weapons are precisely the sort that can dramatically alter the regional military balance when possessed by one country and not its neighbors, the loss of control over their transfer is particularly undesirable.

A second strategic liability inherent in co-production is the danger of inadvertent leakage of exclusive high weapons technology between the superpowers. When a Swedish spy provided the Soviets with a Sidewinder missile, they were able to confirm the precise nature of United States infrared missile homing technology represented in that generation weapon. As more detailed subtechnologies are shared through the co-production process, this kind of leakage becomes easier and more broad-ranging.

As the overall pattern of arms transfers has shifted from the provision of surplus materiel to the sale of modern first-line equipment, it has intruded into the area of nuclear threshold technologies. *Threshold technologies* are systems that can deliver nuclear weapons or facilitate the development of the industrial potential to produce the weapons themselves. India affords the classic example. In 1963, the Indians obtained licensing rights to produce the MiG-21, and the Soviets helped them develop the requisite industrial capabilities. Meanwhile, with the assistance of nuclear power technology provided by Canada, India exploded a nuclear device in August 1974. This unplanned Canadian-Soviet combination has given India the potential to create a nuclear strike capability that could have an ominous impact on the volatile region of South Asia.

The nuclear–conventional force linkage is both a danger and a potential basis for control. One reason that arms limitations in the nuclear arena (although stilll not adequate) have been strikingly more successful than those in the field of conventional armaments is the fact that a virtually worldwide consensus exists regarding the threat that nuclear warfare holds for all humanity. Another reason why it has also been possible to achieve a degree of agreement on nuclear matters is that both the United States and the Soviet Union want to avoid developments that would destabilize their bilateral strategic relationship or precipitate direct confrontation between them. More fundamentally, it is far easier to define strategic stability than stability in conventional force relations; American and Soviet strategists are much more expert at making nuclear calculations and evaluating the impact of nuclear arms control than they are at reckoning the effects of various conventional force levels.

Although nuclear threshold weapons increase the risk of inadvertent nuclear war, only in the most direct and obvious instances, such as in the original United States denial (from which there has been some retreat) of Pershing missiles to Israel, has explicit use been made of this association as a justification for limiting arms transfers. Moreover, many other weapons systems—combat aircraft, ground-to-ground missiles, and certain categories of precision-guided munitions—spill over into the threshold nuclear realm. The producer states' strong collective interest in preventing nuclear war suggests a basis for initiatives by them to structure limitations on transfers of these technologies.

Political-Diplomatic Factors

The calculation that has led producer countries through the years to judge arms transfers to be politically advantageous is reasonably simple. Those countries that either do not want to or cannot produce arms domestically seek them abroad. Those countries capable of exporting arms offer military equipment and related support services, on a grant or sales basis, as one ingredient in the full spectrum of bilateral political relations. As a result, the producer country derives goodwill and some degree of political influence.

When current and anticipated future trends are considered, however, the relationship between arms transfers and political influence appears less direct. First of all, the shift from grants to sales means that arms transfers can engender an entirely different response in the recipient countries. As largesse has given way to contract, the sense of obligation felt by recipients has been diluted; and in an environment in which commercial salespeople from various producer states compete with one another to offer the most attractive terms, arms transactions take on a very matter-of-fact, businesslike character. It is an immutable fact of life that the political leverage resulting from a cash-and-carry deal is in no way comparable to that deriving from massive grants.

In addition, experience has shown that the presence of producer-state personnel in intensely nationalistic recipient countries can have political effects contrary to the desired results. The "Ugly American" is a sociological, not a national, phenomenon.

135

As the Soviets discovered in Egypt, soldiers, sailors, and industrial technicians are not universal ambassadors of goodwill. Similarly, many Americans see initial signs of major difficulty arising in Iran as a consequence of the large number of United States technicians and administrators there. Current programs for the transfer and co-production of sophisticated weapons systems necessitate a decade of highly visible American presence, and this will inevitably lead to competition with the emerging Iranian middle class for scarce housing and consumer goods. As a result, it is just conceivable that, in political terms, the "Iranian connection" could turn out to be a liability rather than an asset.

Ideological Factors

At present, ideology serves mainly to structure the producer community into two competing "sides." This is not an absolutely rigid classification and, from both the recipients' and suppliers' perspectives, it is possible to work both ends of the ideological street. Some observers predict that with the growing predominance of economic motives for arms exports, the ideological division of the market will diminish and cross-bloc transfers will become more common.[7] Relatedly, the loosening of alliance systems and the possibility of greater Soviet-American competition outside the traditional ideological-strategic blocs will increasingly test the importance of ideology in motivating arms sales and in limiting supplier-recipient combinations. Neither Western sales to Yugoslavia nor a growth in Soviet sales to nonsocialist regimes is at all farfetched for the 1980s. Nonetheless, through the early 1980s—probably until the impact of China as a producer is felt—the bipolar ideological distinction will still roughly prevail in the community of producers. Toward the end of the decade, particularly if China becomes a significant arms exporter, competition between China and the Soviet Union for influence over "anti-imperialist" states will alter this pattern, and the role of ideology in arms transfers will grow more complicated and ambiguous.

[7]See the essay by Cahn and Kruzel in this volume, pp. 69–71.

THREE

A Modest Proposal

Too often the literature of arms control is unrealistic, doggedly framing comprehensive programs and final solutions despite the fact that the obstacles to their achievement are virtually insurmountable. In contrast, the underlying concept of the prescription offered here is achievability. The formulation that follows is structured around four major initiatives, each fulfilling a principal requirement for bringing conventional arms transfers under a degree of control, yet couched in terms that take cognizance of the realities likely to prevail in the world of the 1980s. Admittedly, it is an incomplete prescription. Perhaps more than anything else it represents a way station, an intermediate point on the path to more comprehensive control over the producer side of the arms transfers equation. Yet this sort of prescription is important because it endeavors to point the way and suggest practical steps that might be taken to begin the long journey to effective control.

REDIRECTING THE ECONOMIC MOTIVATION BEHIND THE CURRENT DRIVE IN ARMS SALES

The welter of factors—economic, strategic, political, diplomatic, and ideological—that motivate producer countries to promote arms transfers today operates in a complicated pattern of crosscurrents and contradictions and thus is too complex to accommodate any comprehensive program of restraint. The only practical approach is to begin by paring the problem down to where it begins to be more manageable.

One approach to doing so is suggested by the fact that the many economic incentives, though powerful and complicated, are much more dominant within one of the halves of the producer community than within the other. This half, consisting of the United States and the countries of Western Europe, accounted for 59.8 percent of all arms transfers deliveries and over 70 percent of all orders in 1974.[8] To the extent that the Soviet Union and Eastern European producers remain less motivated by economic than by strategic, political, and ideological incentives, economic factors can be addressed within the context of Western exporters' activities; that is, in an area characterized by a higher level of mutual understanding and shared purpose than exists in East-West relations. The consensus of the Atlantic Community on basic ideological and strategic matters makes the differences on economic issues which must be accommodated more amenable to solution.

As noted earlier, one means to damp down the "Gold Rush" mentality influencing competition among Western arms producers might be the creation of some form of North Atlantic common defense market. Such a plan would entail standardization of the design of weapons produced throughout the Atlantic Community and a division of labor in the manufacture of components or entire systems. This latter process of specialization, made possible by standardization, would permit larger production runs and, as a result, greater economics of scale. Although within individual countries certain industries would have to shut down, others would be expanded to serve the Atlantic market without requiring growth in exports to the Third World. While previous efforts at standardization over the years have come to nought, it is possible that with the added incentive of permitting restraint in arms transfers to developing countries, enough previous opponents could be swayed in favor of such an undertaking to make it succeed.

[8]*World Military Expenditures and Arms Transfers, 1965–1974*; also see p. 113 above.

There are three principal reasons for pursuing such an approach. The first is peripheral to the arms transfer problem, although extremely important in its own right. Settling upon common major weapons systems and primary military support hardware for NATO, with production distributed among the member countries of the common defense market on some systematic basis, would bring the arms industries of virtually all the Western producers into a coordinated production scheme and thereby improve the compatibility and combat efficiency of NATO forces. In the process, much redundant research and development could be avoided.

Second, by consolidating production in each specified area (be it communications equipment, wheeled vehicles, electronic components, ammunition, or whatever) in a single country or country pair and guaranteeing those producers the orders of all the member-country armed forces, a number of economic objectives of direct relevance to arms transfers would be achieved. With this kind of specialization, the economic *need* (although not necessarily the desire) to export arms would be reduced or eliminated. Guaranteed access to multiple markets—United States, European, and worldwide—would produce demand of sufficient size that unit-cost factors would be advantageous, minimum economic size would be achieved, and the production base could be kept "warm" without so pressing a need to expand export sales. Moreover, by reducing competition in various weapons categories, the expensive sales promotion activities currently conducted by competitive merchants trying to sell similar weapons in markets outside NATO would be dramatically reduced. To a degree, the present unrestricted buyers' market would be transformed into a sellers' market more conducive to producer restraint on transfers of the more advanced and destabilizing weapons technologies. Lately, specialization, by reducing the number of producers manufacturing similar systems, would severely weaken the frequent bureaucratic rationalization for arms sales: "If we don't sell it to them, they'll just buy it from someone else."

It must be stressed that the decision to restrict arms transfers is ultimately a political one. However, standardization and specialization within NATO—by reducing certain of the economic pressures that prompt governments to export arms—would make it politically easier to argue for restraints, since there could be fewer economic counterarguments.[9]

The third reason for creating an Atlantic common defense market is that the time is propitious. Armed forces continually update their inventories of arms and equipment, of course, but periodically there come times when a major replenishment occurs. We are entering one of those periods right now. Basic decisions regarding what weapons will be deployed and who will produce them are about to establish patterns of production and procurement for the entire next decade. The F-104 combat fighter is being replaced, and the four consortium countries (Belgium, the Netherlands, Denmark, and Norway) have jointly chosen the American F-16 on terms that dictate the manufacture of certain components by the Europeans.[10] The United States is in the throes of modernizing its air defense capability and has purchased the French-German Roland surface-to-air missile as one component of the new-generation short-range air defense (SHORAD) system. Furthermore, the United States has contracted with the Belgians to produce a light machine gun (MAG 58) for use on American tanks in place of the American-manufactured M-60E2. On the other hand, the United States recently announced its final development decision regarding the next-generation main battle tank, awarding the contract to its own Chrysler Corporation rather than to the rival West German manufacturer. While it

[9]Admittedly, such an approach could have certain side effects, some not especially positive. For one, reduced competition could lead to higher costs and lower quality of arms production. A judicious selection of the producer-country pairs, however, based on existing industrial and technological competencies, offers promise of vitality without incurring the penalties of monopolistic waste or brutal market competition. Another side effect is that a common defense market would involve not only government control of international transactions, but also unprecedented government involvement in the defense industries themselves. Governments would have the responsibility for dissolving certain inefficient industries and with the remaining industries depended on to support the entire Western market, there would be a tendency for them to become more highly nationalized than they are today.

[10]See the Cahn and Kruzel essay, p. 75, for more details on this competition.

would have been more dramatic had the United States decided to buy the German Leopard tank outright, the provision for future standardization of major components for the two tanks is nonetheless encouraging. It would be premature to applaud the arrangement yet, but the way is now open to standardize the power plants, track assemblies, and main guns of the next-generation tanks of the NATO countries—with some of the components included on United States versions being European-produced.

Innumerable obstacles, however, confront progress in this regard. The undercurrent of United States–European suspicion and mistrust, which has scuttled all previous efforts at standardization and specialization, remains strong. Despite the Roland and MAG 58 examples, the sentiment persists in the United States that buying European weapons is buying "second class"; yet American willingness to participate in reciprocal arrangements will be crucial to the overall success of the scheme. Maintaining employment and a favorable balance of payments are critical issues for every Western government, and the enormous arms appetites of the oil-producing countries—and the economic benefits that flow from feeding those appetites—will serve to heighten competition and provoke animosities throughout the Atlantic Community. Even if a Western arms producers' condominium is established, producers will still be able to and will, if less compelled, sell arms. And to the extent that the condominium created a sellers' market, it would be viewed with suspicion and chagrin by the community of recipient countries, who would see it as an impediment to their rightful access to the means of self-defense.

Despite these and other difficulties, however, the opportunity to move ahead on a North Atlantic common defense market is genuinely at hand. Probably the most important new ingredient is the changing perception of the likely nature of a war in Europe. As national leaders—even in Washington—become increasingly convinced that sovereignty no longer depends fundamentally on maintaining fully self-contained domestic armaments industries, and as the assertion of this conviction becomes politically possible, then the major stumbling block of the past 15 years will be overcome. A North Atlantic common defense market, with specified sectors of specialization in arms production falling to individual countries or country pairs, would have major economic advantages. It would have the effect of transforming the Western producers' community into something less than an arms cartel, but nonetheless a highly oligopolistic structure.[11] Despite the myriad practical problems involved in the major industrial reallocations required, the practicality of a North Atlantic common defense market should not be dismissed prematurely. Some such scheme of agreed-to specialization in the pattern of production—one that could reduce the economic incentives making arms sales necessary for some countries—is essential if any significant control over the worldwide sale of armaments is to be established.

Even with the kind of coordinated Western production arrangement envisaged here, reducing the magnitude of total arms transfers to countries outside the area would not be without cost. To illustrate, consider two hypothetical scenarios: one in which sales outside NATO are decreased (as a result of conscious restraint) but sales within NATO are held constant; another in which sales outside NATO are consciously decreased but production and purchases within NATO are increased, either for security reasons or to offset the aggregate effects on the arms industries in the alliance. Under the first scenario, with other factors remaining constant, the overall level of arms production (and jobs) would decrease, and the balance-of-payments position for Western exporters as a whole would deteriorate. Under the second scenario, no jobs would be lost, but the overall Western balance of payments would still suffer (not to mention the political implications of such a force buildup for the East-West balance in Europe).

Still, while the costs of restraining arms transfers cannot be eliminated, structuring the Western producer community into a coordinated condominium would establish a much better posture from which a strategy of restraining transfer of at least the more

[11] For a full development of the concept of the North Atlantic common defense market, see Thomas A. Callaghan, Jr., *US/European Cooperation in Military and Civilian Technology*, Center for Strategic and International Studies, Georgetown University, Washington, D.C., September 1975.

sensitive types of weapons could be put into practice. Such a strategy of restraint is by no means preordained. Consolidation of the North Atlantic producer community makes it feasible, but in the absence of a conscious political choice to impose stringent governmental limitations, the arms trade could just as easily increase as decrease. The kind of consolidated scheme envisaged here provides a sufficiently broad market within the North Atlantic Community to sustain selected, economically viable defense industries in each country. However, one cannot expect the corporations concerned to be content with just the volume of business resulting from NATO sales. Reducing the need for arms sales does not guarantee any reduction in the desire for them. Restraint will depend upon governmental determination.

As a final note, it is appropriate to address the question, How do you get there from here? Standardization and specialization within the North Atlantic Community will have economic effects that are different, and often directly opposite, for an economy as a whole and for individual economic sectors. In overall national or aggregate terms, the loss of modest tank and aircraft production in exchange for massive business in communications equipment might well be advantageous, or at least not disadvantageous, in its effects on total employment and the balance of payments. For the tank and aircraft corporations involved, though, for the people employed by them, and for the politicians in whose districts they are located, the prospect of such a trade-off is enormously threatening. Indeed, the political rigor mortis triggered by such prospects, as much as any other single factor, has obstructed any real progress to date.

This important fact of life cannot be ignored. The solution lies in political leaders facing up to the dislocations involved and creating programs of compensation and adjustment assistance as integral elements of any standardization proposal. The compensatory programs would undoubtedly have to involve governmental offset spending to create new jobs, a full array of information, relocation and retraining services, and augmented unemployment benefits for displaced workers. Such steps are all straightforward and practicable. What is required is that national leaders see the benefits as important enough to warrant mounting the campaigns necessary to bring them about.

143

STRUCTURING PRODUCER RESTRAINT
ON A REGIONAL BASIS

Governments all over the globe are arming themselves at an unprecedented rate. World military spending, now almost $300 billion per year, is 45 percent higher in constant dollars than it was in 1960. Because of the quantum pulse of petrodollar spending, it is occasionally suggested that the "arms sales problem" is really a "Persian Gulf problem," that efforts to restrain arms transfers are worthwhile only in the Middle East.

The preeminence of petroleum-financed arms orders is obvious, and by any calculation Middle East demand is destined to remain predominant through the 1980s. The Gulf is, in fact, a supercritical area: the intractable and nearby Arab-Isareli dispute is affected by the arms race there, and the region is fast becoming the scene of major superpower competition. With enormous oil-based buying power currently unchecked, it can legitimately be considered the key region with regard to arms transfers.

But one must not allow the enormity of the Middle East problem to eclipse the important dangers and opportunities that exist in other regions. The relatively small volume of arms transfers to Latin American and sub-Saharan Africa, for example, represents a genuine opportunity for preclusive restraint. The feasibility of nonarmament is so much greater than that of disarmament that these opportunities should not be overlooked.

Unfortunately, the small volume of arms imports frequently causes leaders in these regions, and the world at large, to dismiss the issue as one of little urgency. But it is urgent. In some regions, time may be running out. The tension between the vast black majority and the white-minority-dominated regimes of South Africa and Rhodesia continues to grow, and the chances of avoiding armed conflict appear bleak. The Angolan experience has brought some increased attention and concern to the question of arms imports, but no formal or informal regional or subregional arms limitation proposals have been made.

Similar dangers threaten other regions of the world. Intense local rivalries persist, among them, India versus Pakistan, North versus South Korea, Brazil versus Argentina, Greece versus

Turkey, Kenya versus Uganda, Algeria versus Morocco, and Ethiopia versus Somalia. Regional arms races in these areas serve only to heighten local tensions, and the outbreak of regional conflicts retards and complicates economic development. Thus a coordination of producers' arms transfer policies, aimed at restraining arms flows to all factions in such conflict-prone regions, would be a constructive and practical approach.

Much work will have to be done to put such a coordinated scheme into effect. First of all, it will be necessary to determine what criteria should be used by producers in evaluating security conditions within a given region. Obviously, judgments concerning the desired level, composition, and distribution of arms can be made only with respect to some set of standards and objectives, such as preserving regional power balances, preventing wars, and confining the scope or limiting the severity of the destructiveness of wars if they cannot be prevented. In regions where one power enjoys a margin of military superiority, owing to earlier imports or home production superiority, for example, arms transfers could be restricted to the weaker states so as to redress the imbalance. Exporters to unstable regions could restrict arms transfers to defensive weapons systems (to the extent that they can be distinguished from offensive systems), or at least to those systems that would not give the recipients the capability to execute a massive surprise attack against their neighbors.

Suppliers might agree to refrain from providing states in a particular region with advanced weapons that have not yet made an appearance anywhere in that region. Thus, attack aircraft whose performance exceeds certain specified parameters (range, speed, payload, etc.) might be denied all states of a region unless one state had acquired such systems. Surface-to-surface missiles might similarly be kept out of many regions. In the event that a state from a given region resorts to home production or turns to a nonparticipating exporter (the Soviet Union being the obvious candidate), restrictions on the rest of the region would have to be relaxed. Indeed, as a disincentive to violating the regional restrictions, the exporters might declare their preparedness to provide compensatory arms at advantageous terms to the neighbors of violators. Relatively tranquil regions, often overlooked by arms controllers by virtue of their tranquility, in which supplier restraint might work well include Central America, West Africa, and Central Africa. More troubled areas for which many advanced weapons might nonetheless still be proscribed include the Maghreb, Southeast Asia, and South America.

Next, the question must be addressed as to how limitations on arms transfers within particular regions can be institutionalized. Should the controls be implemented and enforced through existing regional bodies or organizations or through independent machinery set up exclusively for this purpose? What pressures can be brought to bear on exporters who fail to comply? In addition, how can restriction be enforced at all in regions where both Western and Eastern producers supply arms? And even where Eastern exporters have not been previously active, will states of the region not turn to them in the event that Western restraint is imposed? Whenever possible, it would be highly desirable to seek some sort of involvement by all who act as suppliers, although in some instances (the Middle East, for example) this might prove to be unworkable.

Initiatives from within a given region are unquestionably the best basis on which to build programs to restrict the influx of arms. It may take prompting from the producer states, however, to get the process started. In any event, the means of controlling arms transfers is almost certain to differ from region to region. From the producer-country perspective, the approach should be one that provides worldwide coverage but consists of a series of distinct regional policies, specifically tailored to the very different requirements and opportunities present in each region.[12]

JOINT CREATION OF PARTIAL RESTRAINTS BY WESTERN AND SOVIET–EAST EUROPEAN PRODUCERS

One of the most perplexing problems in any producer-oriented attempt to control conventional arms transfers is the presence of alternative suppliers. As noted earlier, except for the most

[12]For a detailed discussion of the possibilities for regional *recipient* restraints, see the essay by Jacques Huntzinger in this volume, pp. 163–197.

sophisticated and elaborate military systems (nuclear-powered submarines, aircraft carriers, supersonic bombers, etc.), most armaments can be produced by a large number of countries. The ranks of the producers and the technological range of their production capability will continue to grow during the 1980s. Even more pointedly, when Soviet and Eastern European producers line up in competition with Western producers, each side possesses the capacity to produce the full range of weapons and military equipment. It is obvious, therefore, that any attempt at bringing conventional arms transfers under control which does not to some extent involve the producers on both sides would be at best fragile and at worst abortive. For instance, the initiative of exporter restraint on a region-by-region basis, just discussed, would be very vulnerable if Eastern exporters refused to cooperate or acquiesce.

Given the very real strategic, political, and ideological differences between East and West, the basis for mutual action is unfortunately limited. Some experimentation in East-West exporter cooperation is necessary. There are at least two important areas in which shared concern over the consequences of arms transfers appears to outweigh the attraction of unilateral gain: regional nuclear war and terrorism employing miniature, precision-guided munitions. Each of these areas of shared concern offers a certain basis for restraining the transfer of selected categories of arms and perhaps for gaining the rudimentary experience required for more substantial East-West cooperation on restricting arms transfers later.

Restraining Transfers of Nuclear Threshold Technologies

The record of the great powers' willingness to seek arrangements for limitation and control in the nuclear field, while by no means an unqualified success, offers a striking contrast to their record in the realm of conventional arms. The Nuclear Non-Proliferation Treaty (NPT), the Strategic Arms Limitation Talks (SALT) accords, the recent Threshold Test Ban Treaty, and collaboration in the London nuclear suppliers conference have no conventional counterparts. The conviction of the Soviets and the Ameri-

147

cans—and, indeed, the consensus among most producer states—
that the outbreak of nuclear warfare would jeopardize the entire
world is a rare case of genuine shared purpose in the international
arena.

The common interest in preventing regional nuclear conflict
provides an opportunity to foster a degree, albeit a modest
degree, of cooperation in the field of conventional arms transfers
as well, in the form of limits on transfers of so-called nuclear
threshold technologies. Some of the systems included in this
category, specifically high-performance fighter-bombers, have
such broad utility in nonnuclear contexts that it probably is not
possible to restrain their supply on the basis of their "threshold"
potential. Other weapons, however, particularly the more sophisticated ground-to-ground missiles, have such limited utility in
non-nuclear roles that it is practical to treat them as "nuclear
adjunct" systems.

The tacit agreement between the superpowers to control the
provision of ground-to-ground missiles to their clients in the
Arab-Israeli conflict is moderately encouraging. Although the
Russians equipped Egypt with Scud missiles, they did not supplement them with newer, more sophisticated systems. The
United States, in turn, resisted repeated appeals by Israel during
and after the 1973 War for the Pershing missile system.

Restraint in the provision of these missile systems to the
Middle East may be more symbolic than actual, since Egypt,
Syria, and Israel all have supersonic aircraft capable of delivering
nuclear weapons, and Israel is producing its own Jericho missile.
The significant point, however, is that the United States and the
Soviet Union apparently share the desire to limit the likelihood of
regional nuclear conflict and have shown some willingness to
behave accordingly in a region where they have otherwise shown
little restraint. There are other regional confrontations that both
the United States and the Soviet Union would clearly like to keep
from crossing the nuclear threshold and in which the pressures on
the superpowers to export without restraint are less than in the
Middle East; the escalating white-black hostilities in Southern
Africa, the Indo-Pakistani conflict, and the North-South confrontation in Korea are three examples. In South Asia in particular,

where India has already detonated its own nuclear device, the potential for nuclear miscalculation is great and the denial of missile delivery systems might cool the nuclear fever now burning in that part of the world.

The superpowers' calculus is never straightforward in such situations. For example, it is possible that the Soviets might willingly accept the increased danger of war between India and Pakistan leading to the use of nuclear weapons (which they, in any case, may consider a highly unlikely outcome), in order to see India equipped with missiles that would constitute a regional nuclear threat to China. Despite the complexities involved, however, there is sufficient agreement between the superpowers to serve as a reasonable basis for developing arrangements to restrain the transfer of sophisticated ground-to-ground nuclear-capable missiles. Such missiles are expensive to develop and complicated to produce. The United States and the Soviet Union are the paramount suppliers, with France, West Germany, and Japan potential producers, but ones who share similar apprehensions regarding the prospect of nuclear war. The other prospective producer during the 1980s is China, but the uncertainty as to future Chinese policy makes it difficult to predict the impact of China as an alternative producer. One cannot dismiss the possibility that China would balance whatever the Soviets provided to India with transfers to Pakistan. However, even if China were unwilling to cooperate with other arms producers, limiting the field to one uncontrolled supplier would seem to be an improvement over a generally uncontrolled environment, if only because it would constrain importers and eliminate competition that leads to imprudent arms transfers.

Restraining Transfers of Miniature, Precision-Guided Munitions

A second area in which the beginnings of a consensus appear to exist among producers is that involving the transfer of miniature, precision-guided munitions to nongovernmental, terrorist groups. As in the case of the relationship between threshold technologies and regional nuclear conflict, what causes this ar-

149

mament domain to take on a particularly threatening caste is its potential for unpredictability and indiscretion. The danger was epitomized by the 1974 Palestinian plot to down a commercial airliner in Rome by means of a Soviet SA-7 Grail hand-held, heat-seeking anti-aircraft missile. Were Arab terrorists the only potential customers, the interest in controlling the transfer of these precision-guided munitions might be decidedly one-sided. The fact is, of course, that there are reactionary as well as revolutionary terrorist groups, not to mention extremists among the nationalities within the Soviet Union. The prospect of numerous terrorist splinter groups, of varying political persuasions, with ready access to hand-held anti-aircraft missiles, randomly blackmailing and assassinating by attacking commercial airliners, is an alarming specter to all who produce these weapons—not to mention all who fly!

The 1980s will see this domain grow increasingly difficult to control, perhaps even within the Eastern bloc. The technology involved in heat-seeking missiles is already well known, and the only real obstacle to widespread production is the technological complexity and high cost of miniaturization. But co-production is already within the grasp of Iran, and China surely will have weapons of this sort in production within 10 years. The best prospect for control lies in solidifying the consensus that, on the basis of sheer common sense, transfers of miniature, precision-guided munitions should be severely restrained, or at least tightly regulated. Only if producers block the distribution of these weapons and refuse to establish co-production arrangements for them can a totally unsatisfactory environment be averted.

In both of these instances—nuclear threshold technologies and miniature, precision-guided munitions—the *process* of control is as important as the fact of it. Restraining the proliferation of weapons in these categories would be advantageous in its own right in terms of promoting a more moderate world order. Just as important, it would afford a basis on which to construct procedures and instrumentalities through which the two major strategic antagonists could define and pursue more far-reaching mutual objectives in the realm of conventional arms transfers— particularly the establishment of a comprehensive system of restraint based on weapons categories.

It would be vain to presume that simply bringing together producers from East and West to discuss conventional arms transfers would automatically lead to the resolution of their basic differences. No such magic exists. By the same token, there are instances in which a genuine mutuality of interest in restraining arms transfers is present. Unfortunately, the tortured history and complex web of competition between the two superpowers often prevent them from acting upon that mutual interest. The clear benefits of genuine collaboration in nuclear threshold technologies and miniature, precision-guided munitions offer some promise of overcoming that legacy and making these domains of conflict less threatening.

Restraining Retransfers by Arms Recipients

Modern technology advances at a lightning pace, and even weapons of moderate sophistication tend to become outdated before they wear out. As a result, those near the top of the military totem pole are moved to replace their current inventories with new models, and seek to defray some of the growing costs of modernization by exporting their present stocks.

The retransfer by recipient countries of earlier years' arms purchases is not a new aspect of the arms transfers landscape, but two factors have caused it to acquire increased importance. The first is the accelerated "pulse" of arms sales, occasioned largely by petrodollar orders, combined with the apparent likelihood throughout the 1980s of an increased propensity on the part of nonproducers to purchase arms. This means that a great deal of military equipment in or destined for inventories is preordained to become obsolescent before it really grows old. The quantity of arms involved and the enormity of the price tag create an irresistible incentive for recipients who wish to modernize their forces to recover some of the cost of their earlier investments through resales.

The second factor is the new circumstances surrounding military sales today. Recipients are no longer naturally inclined toward slavish compliance with restrictions imposed by producers on the subsequent disposition of armaments. When arms transfers primarily took the form of grants and the number of potential suppliers among whom to choose and bargain was severely limited, producers could exercise a reasonable degree of control over the end use and retransfer of the military items provided. Today, with the great majority of transfers being cash sales and with orders being placed with whatever supplier offers the most attractive contract, producer leverage is reduced.

Paradoxically, while the ability of producers to restrict the retransfer of arms is decreasing, the need for control is becoming all the more crucial. With so much of the current arms trade and that projected for the 1980s consisting of first-line, modern equipment, today's recipients are accumulating inventories that will retain impressive effectiveness—especially in certain regional settings—long after even newer, more effective generations of arms are developed. Current recipients interested in continuously updating their forces will find many eager recipients for their older but still potent stocks.

The extent of restraint currently imposed by producers over the retransfer of arms varies considerably. Both the United States and the Soviet Union are very restrictive, requiring as a precondition to approval of the sale assurances that recipients will not transfer the equipment without prior consent. By contrast, France customarily imposes no retransfer limitations whatsoever. It has been recommended that all producers make a prerequisite to any arms transfer the acceptance by recipients of retransfer and end-use restraints, and further that a standardized form be approved and employed in all transactions to certify and formalize the restrictions.[13] Recognizing the natural inclination of recipients to modernize their military inventories and their need to sell off current arms holdings in order to do so, other observers have suggested that producers include in arms sales contracts provisions to buy back the weapons or create incentives for recipient countries to scrap armaments rather than resell them.[14]

[13]John Stanley and Maurice Pearton, *The International Trade in Arms*, Praeger Publishers, New York, 1972.

[14]Lewis A. Frank, *The Arms Trade in International Relations*, Praeger Publishers, New York, 1969, and William B. Bader, "The Proliferation of Conventional Weapons," in Cyril E. Black and Richard A. Falk, *The Future of the International Legal Order*, vol. III, *Conflict Management*, Princeton University Press, Princeton, N.J., 1971.

While these are sensible, indeed important suggestions, it is not very likely that they will be generally accepted and implemented in the arms transfers environment of the 1980s. Consequently, partial solutions might be sought. Although it is unlikely that all producers, East and West, will agree to impose ironclad retransfer restrictions, it is entirely imaginable that if a North Atlantic common defense market developed, such restraints could be applied to all of the group's arms sales. With the reduced competition that would result from the common defense market, arms buyers could no longer play one producer off against another for more relaxed retransfer provisions. It might also prove possible to achieve restraints from the recipient side. For example, the countries of Latin America, sub-Saharan Africa, or some subregional element collectively could agree to require "buy back" provisions in all contracts for arms sales in their area in exchange for acceptance of resale restrictions. Alternatively, the most opportune approach might be for the producers to isolate certain types of weapons systems (such as precision-guided munitions, tanks, or combat aircraft) and formulate arrangements to control their retransfer. Or, the superpowers could impose binding retransfer restrictions on sales of those sophisticated weapons systems that only they can provide.

It is not enough simply to design comprehensive schemes that would be helpful only if everyone elected to abide by them. The retransfer market must be analyzed carefully and continually, with respect to patterns of producers, geographic groupings, and categories of weapons systems, so as to find the various combinations that offer real opportunities for control. No tidy or all-inclusive plan is likely to be achievable in the 1980s. But retransfers need to be recognized as a key category of the arms transfers problem, one demanding priority attention, and control should be sought through whatever means offer realistic opportunities.

FOUR

The Longer-Term Prospects for Producer Restraint

What lies beyond the initial steps and partial solutions just described? Ultimately, how much can be achieved through producer restraint? Toward the end of the 1980s and beyond, will further refinement and elaboration of arrangments for producer restraint be able to bring conventional arms transfers under effective control? If so, what are the major requirements to be met?

A good deal of the preceding discussion has centered around how economic factors influence producer countries to export arms and military equipment. Several steps have been suggested to reshape the pattern of economic incentives in such a way that conventional arms transfers might be promoted less energetically. Promoting a new and more realistic awareness that across-the-board self-reliance in arms production no longer constitutes the foundation of national sovereignty has been advocated. This would facilitate standardization and specialization among Western producers and, by so doing, serve as a precursor for reducing the force of certain economic incentives and strengthening the basis for direct restraining action.

The essence of effective long-term producer restraint is the realization, formally or tacitly, of an association of all arms producers—Warsaw Pact, North Atlantic Community, and second-tier—through which the levels of arms transfers can be negotiated and constrained. Within this producer community, as noted previously, the practical counterincentives to exporting arms differ from group to group. There is no simple formula for reconciling those differences, but efforts must continue to be made to search out combinations of shared interest and patterns of mutual purpose on which to build agreements to limit arms transfers. Unfortunately, the internal pressures for expanded social programs and these programs' increasing cost, as well as the continuing pressure of rising raw material costs, place immense financial pressure on producer-country governments, forcing them to sustain, and work to increase, their export earnings. Under these circumstances, the suggestion that arms exports be reduced is not particularly popular.

The point is repeatedly made in the literature of arms control that arms transfers represent only a small percentage of total exports, and so producer countries can afford to reduce them. No doubt this is theoretically true. Unfortunately, in an environment of sustained economic tension, with tight budgets, vociferous domestic pressure groups, and a decidedly less-than-benign international environment, the incentives to do so are hard to marshal. Doing so is not impossible, of course, but it is difficult.

Some advocates seem to think the solution lies in transforming the arms trade: turning away from exporting tanks and airplanes and emphasizing instead increased exports of agricultural and industrial equipment and services. Implementing such an approach would involve, among other things, major programs of industrial diversification and resource reallocation. The task would be an intimidating one. Several studies of actual attempts at diversification have been conducted over the past 13 years by the ACDA.[15] What seems, in theory, to be a manageable transition has proven in practice to entail major obstacles and dislocations. Marketing departments, in particular, have required near-total restructuring and reorientation. Of the commerical diversification attempts studied, "failure was more frequent than success."[16] Most efforts at diversification also involve increased public costs (tax rebates, long-term loans and loan guarantees, joint industry-government financing, etc.). Financially hard-pressed govern-

[15] For example, see *The Economic Impact of Reductions in Defense Spending*, U.S. Arms Control and Disarmament Agency, Washington, D.C., 1972.
[16] Ibid., p. 9.

CONVENTIONAL ARMS TRANSFERS AND CONTROL

ments may not consider this a viable alternative. Furthermore, the revenue from sales of military hardware is so much greater than that from exports of agricultural implements that the latter are, in fact, not even remote substitutes in terms of their balance-of-payments effects. The price of one F-14 would keep most developing countries in agricultural machinery for years. Moreover, developing countries do not need sophisticated agricultural equipment, but cheap, rugged machines that many will be increasingly capable of producing for themselves.

Beyond the economics of the situation, achieving more than modest, incremental reductions in conventional arms transfers, and making those reductions stick, will require joint commitment and resolve on the part of recipients and producers alike. While this essay addresses the issue of controlling conventional arms transfers from the producer side, the subject cannot be satisfactorily dealt with from that perspective alone. Every producer restraint arrangement includes some recipient involvement. The more comprehensive the arrangement, and the more likely it is to work, the greater that mutual involvement becomes. In this endeavor, a body of procedures and institutional machinery is required so that arms transfer issues can be discussed on a systematic and continuous basis.

Achieving the necessary mutual action rests to a large degree in the hands of the recipients. But by the same token enough is known about the recipient community and its orientation to indicate that the willingness of its members to limit their accumulation of arms depends, in part, on the willingness of the producer states to do likewise. So long as the producers persist in amassing ever more potent armed forces and stockpiles of conventional armaments, the recipient states will be inclined to consider producer initiatives to restrain arms transfers as disingenuous maneuvers designed to keep them in a situation of permanent inferiority.

It is difficult to be optimistic that producer states will reverse current escalatory trends in their own conventional arms capabilities during the 1980s. Strategic nuclear parity between the superpowers and global fear of nuclear conflict have made reliance on conventional armed forces even more pronounced. The

157

Mutual Force Reduction (MFR) talks in Vienna show little promise of producing any major breakthrough; and even though some success may be achieved in that regard during the next decade and a half, there is no indication that sustained and cumulative conventional force reductions are in the offing.

Ironically, this recipient-producer linkage has the effect of tying what is generally conceded to be the more achievable task, nonarmament in the recipient community, to a less achievable one, disarmament among producer states. The extreme complexity of conventional disarmament, particularly when it involves the superpowers during a period when their nuclear forces offset one another and accentuate the importance of conventional competition, makes one pessimistic in candidly appraising the long-term prospects for the restraint of arms transfers.

It is hoped that the foregoing discussion will prove overly pessimistic. Countries have many other needs beyond acquiring more and better armaments. Leaders throughout the world, in countries that produce arms as well as in those that purchase them, recognize that arms expenditures compete for the resources needed to address those other concerns. In the words of one commentator, "The consequent denial of resources to efforts which attack the traditional enemies of mankind, such as ignorance, hunger, and disease, emphasizes again the imperative need for progress in both nuclear and conventional arms control agreements."[17]

Throughout this essay I have suggested that progress in restraining world arms trade could gradually acquire momentum as modest initial successes lead to greater trust and confidence and more ambitious efforts. But the harsh reality must be faced that the prospects for producer restraint of arms transfers may fade over time, and that early successes will give way to frustrations as deeper, more significant measures are tried. Rather than representing a way station on the route to effective control, the partial arrangements described in Chapter 3 might constitute the peak of opportunities for producer restraint in the 1980s. It could

[17]John Culver, "Needed: A More Realistic and Informed Defense Debate," U.S. Congress, Senate, Press Release, March 1976, p. 1.

be that, at best, the initiatives for producer restraint presented here will offer a chance for only a temporary period of relief from the headlong rush toward world armament. If that respite is not capitalized upon by the achievement of significant advances on the recipient side of the arms transfers equation, the opportunity for comprehensive restraint may slip away and, fueled by an expanded number of producer states, a new spate of world arms stockpiling could ensue. Concern over the prospect of that undesirable possibility should be no excuse, however, for not implementing the initial measures of producer restraint proposed here.

Regional Recipient Restraints

Jacques Huntzinger

ONE

Emphasis on Demand

INTRODUCTION

The growth of world arms trade has two fundamental sources: the proliferation of independent nation-states and the international division of labor as it relates to those areas of industrial activity that are important to the production of weapons. The first factor creates "appetites" for conventional arms outside the developed world, owing to the burgeoning desire of a hundred new national entities to build at least adequate military establishments. The second factor amplifies the first: the industrialized world has the means and experience of production, the established military-industrial complexes, and the market incentives to arm the countries of the developing world.

The traditional distinction between "developed" supplier and ."developing" recipient will become less clear in the 1980s. New producers outside the industrialized world are already emerging at the regional level. And traffic within the industrialized world will be heavy both among producers in the Western camp and among the European socialist countries. Most industrialized states will thus become producer-recipients and may create among themselves regional markets based on a degree of specialization. Nevertheless, the principal producers of today—the United States, the Soviet Union, France, Great Britain, West

NOTE: This essay, translated from the French original by Alexander R. Vershbow, was edited and adapted for publication by David C. Gompert.

Germany, Canada, Italy, Japan, Sweden, Switzerland, and China—will remain so tomorrow. And the recipients of conventional arms will remain heavily concentrated in Europe and the Third World.

European arms trade questions must be viewed in the context of the general course of East-West relations. In Europe, the role and importance of conventional arms depend largely on the attitudes and interests of the superpowers, their bilateral relationship, the evolving structures and doctrines of the two great military alliances, and the role of nuclear weapons in the continent's heart. Europe is an overarmed but stable region; its stability depends essentially on factors well beyond the importation of arms by its nations, East and West.

In contrast, in the Third World the quantity and quality of available—largely imported—conventional arms constitute the factors most basic to the security of individual states and regions. The Third World, generally speaking, is and will remain in the 1980s an unstable zone caught up in a process of accelerating militarization, a zone predisposed toward the acquisition of conventional arms. In this respect, conventional arms proliferation throughout the Third World poses particular risks and dilemmas largely absent and not widely appreciated in the industrialized world.

During the cold war, the main arteries of international arms flow linked the United States with Europe and East Asia, the two principal security theaters abutting the communist world. Arms were not sold but given in the interest of strengthening the first line of defense against the Soviet camp. Until approximately 1960, arms transfers were divided about evenly between developed and developing countries, conforming to patterns of East-West security concerns rather than to relative stages of national political and economic development.

Since the mid-1960s, arms trade with the developing countries has constituted three-fourths of the world total; and in the period 1967–1971 three-fourths of the Third World imports were concentrated in Asia (the two Vietnams, the two Koreas) and the Middle East (Egypt, Syria, Israel). Since 1973, the focus of demand has shifted even more toward the Middle East, owing to reduced

American commitments in Indochina and to the Yom Kippur War. Military expenditures among the developing countries grew from $15 billion in 1960 to $39 billion in 1975. While Latin America increased its spending twofold in this period, the Middle East increased its spending eightfold. And the growth has recently accelerated: from 1973 to 1974, Third World arms spending rose 40 percent; it rose 50 percent in the Middle East alone, thanks to the huge payments surpluses among the oil producers of the Persian Gulf. "Deliveries made to the Middle East in the last years are such that the groups of countries of this region can deploy 2,300 combat aircraft and 10,500 armored vehicles, at a time when there are 3,000 planes and 12,250 armored vehicles in Europe."[1]

The specific reasons for the upsurge in demand for arms in a given region of course vary. But in general, strong demand has developed in the Third World since 1960 because, in contrast with countries in Europe, most developing countries were not yet saturated with weapons and would require a good two decades to reach a comparable level of militarization. Many former colonial states had virtually no defense forces when they attained independence, and so required a heavy infusion of arms imports to reach the force levels consistent with their new status. Third World security and power politics are not governed by the rules and constraints of nuclear deterrence and the awesome presence of the superpowers, and the possession of conventional arms translates more directly into usable national power. Indeed, unlike the state of Europe, most developing countries want arms for reasons largely unrelated to East-West security; their demand has therefore not subsided as détente has flourished. Conventional arms will continue to play a greater role in the Third World than in Europe in the 1980s, especially if nuclear proliferation proves—as I believe it will—to be more limited than is expected today. So the classical rules of the game, and classical uses of force, will remain highly relevant in the Third World. Conventional arms will be the key to national power and hegemony, to

[1] *Arms Trade Registers: The Arms Trade with the Third World*, Stockholm International Peace Research Institute (SIPRI), 1975.

regional balances or imbalances of power, to coercion and local conflicts.

Above all, conventional arms are needed, particularly by the newer states, for establishing a national defense. So long as every state wishes to have the capability at least to assure its self-defense, the future is bright for manufacturers of fighter planes, tanks, and armored vehicles. But conventional arms, unlike nuclear weapons, are multifunctional: they can be used in a whole gamut of conflicts and crises, diverse in nature and scale. They facilitate, albeit at great cost, the satisfaction of many objectives of new states: prestige, independence, power, security, and the maintenance of domestic order. They will be sought for regional preponderance, influence, and expansion and for the preservation or restoration of balances of power in potentially unstable and conflict-prone regions. Finally, there are purely internal factors influencing new states to acquire conventional arms: desires to suppress internal subversion and secession; to maintain urban and rural order; and to satisfy budding military complexes (more "military-bureaucratic" than "military-industrial") whose support is vital to the survival of political regimes.

Many arms trade experts contend that the industrialized producer states stimulate demand in the consumer states. Some attribute this pressure from the supply side to the basic elements of imperialist domination over the Third World; others feel that the scale and political power of the military-industrial complexes in the developed states encourage the cultivation of export markets to maintain production growth. These theories stress the role of supply over that of demand in shaping markets and driving the arms trade. Other analysts emphasize the growing dependence of buyers on suppliers as stemming from rising production costs and continuous technological advances that make it very hard for the Third World states to produce their own sophisticated armaments. Even the capacity of the medium-rank producing states to compete with the major exporters will become increasingly limited, owing to the growing divergence between the military research and development budgets of the great powers and those of the medium powers. The latter will have more and more difficulty producing in all areas of weapons technology. Thus, transactions between the great producing powers[2] and the Third World will increasingly dominate the market. As a consequence, the developing states' dependence on a few key producers will be accentuated.

Given the preponderance of a few producers, many analysts believe that effective regulation of arms trade must involve the imposition of limitations on exports. There has been much discussion of the possibility of guidelines for conventional arms control being designed by the superpowers to regulate sales of sophisticated weaponry, to restrict total sales or sales of certain types of systems, or to restrain transfers to a particular region. But in this study we begin with the propostion that the demand for arms in the Third World will continue growing whatever the policies of the producer states. The wants and needs of the states of the Third World will be such that the regulation of exports will be a difficult enterprise with limited effect. The magnitude of demand will impede efforts to institute restraint among the exporters and, even in the event of a more restricted world market, will lead to expanded indigenous production in the Third World, thereby reducing the ability of the great powers to exercise moderating leverage and to contribute to the maintenance of regional balances. It is therefore necessary to consider whether, where, and under what conditions it would be possible to restrain and regulate demand itself, recognizing that the long-term goal should be the establishment of a dual arms control system involving cooperation among industrial producer states coordinated with rules established among Third World states.

ALTERNATIVE APPROACHES TO LIMITING THE DEMAND FOR ARMS

There are four basic approaches to restraining the demand for arms: unilateral, global, bilateral, and regional.

Unilateral restrictions on demand—action by an acquisitor of arms to institute rules of "self-restraint"—can take a number of

---

[2]That is, the United States and the Soviet Union, with the next echelon (France and Great Britain) barely holding their own.

167

different forms. A state can decide to refrain from acquiring a given weapons system and in fact codify this self-denial as a constitutional or legislative rule. Two living examples of such restrictions are the Japanese constitution, which prohibits both nuclear weapons and "offensive" forces, and the translation into the West German constitution of international agreements on nuclear weapons and certain biological and chemical weapons. It is unlikely in the extreme that such constitutional self-restrictions could be widely and credibly adopted in the conventional arms area; the rather special contexts of the German and Japanese restrictions hardly provide a precedent that could be generalized.

Another more realistic approach to limiting demand unilaterally is the establishment by governments of administrative, juridical, and financial rules and procedures affecting arms imports. Under such an approach, imports of military materials would be subject to strict internal review processes: import quota procedures, special systems for justification and authorization by competent governmental organs, etc. The establishment of such regulations in individual Third World states—or, for that matter, in any state—would constitute progress. But these measures would be an act of determined political will to restrain arms imports and would survive only as long as that political will—or the domestic alignment that produced it—survived. It would be very difficult for a government to embark on this enterprise if there were any likelihood that the regulations would adversely affect national security. Such measures would not be adopted by states until a favorable local security climate existed—indeed, a climate that would permit, or perhaps only be made possible by, arms control success beyond the unilateral level.

A more classical approach—the *global approach*—involves measures that can be established by treaty among both consumer and producer states of the international community. One could, of course, conceive of an undertaking like the Nuclear Non-Proliferation Treaty (NPT) in the conventional sphere. Just as the NPT draws a distinction—though a hard one to maintain in practice—between military and civilian nuclear technologies, a conventional replica might apply only to certain sensitive weapons (such as bombers, tanks, missiles).

But who can seriously envisage such an enterprise being undertaken in the coming years? It would be necessary to limit the scope of the treaty to those weapons systems that are not considered vital to national security requirements yet are thought to be potentially hazardous to the security of others. But how could states agree on such a list? And would the principal producer states readily accept such a treaty? In any case, a sweeping agreement of this sort would certainly appear arbitrary to individual states, whose dependence upon the world market for certain systems may be quite justifiable in the face of a rival whose accumulated stocks or home production capacity was considered excessive. Yet establishing different restrictions for different states would be inherently discriminatory, unmanageable in practice, and probably impossible to negotiate.

A more modest type of global approach based on information-exchange and publicity processes could be institutionalized internationally. Until now the sole means the UN has had to influence international arms trade has been such publicity—specifically, publishing a record of international arms transfers.[3] The idea is that publicizing all transactions permits international bodies, third-party governments, and world media and public opinion to blunt, through embarrassment and diplomatic pressure, the demands of buyer states. It would of course be desirable that the information system provide worldwide coverage and that all transactions be effectively monitored, recorded, and reported. But this plan presumes that states would no longer link the notions of security and secrecy as they do today. Moreover, the dissuasive effect of international publicity has yet to be proved; recent major arms transactions have received considerable publicity, and the damping effect on international traffic has, so far at least, not been impressive. Thus, one can see difficulties with even this very modest multilateral approach, although it is possible to envisage such initiatives being accepted by states in the 1980s.

The *bilateral approach* to the regulation of arms trade might

---

[3]The Stockholm International Peace Research Institute (SIPRI) and the United States Arms Control and Disarmament Agency (ACDA) also provide comprehensive public reporting of arms transactions.

center on the inclusion of regulatory stipulations in the agreements and contracts by which states procure arms. One example of this is the French-Libyan agreement, according to which Libya is forbidden to use the Mirage fighters purchased from France in foreign theaters and to lend these planes to other states. The regulation does not restrict acquisition but only the conditions of subsequent use of the purchased material. In this particular case, the Libyans have been less than faithful to their obligations. The United States and the Soviet Union have also included restrictive clauses in bilateral transfer agreements, though again, there have been breaches in implementation, as in the case of Turkey's use of United States arms in the invasion of Cyprus.

Still, such an approach to rule making seems conducive to expansion. "Umbrella agreements" could be established bilaterally between suppliers and recipients, fixing for future transactions ceilings on purchases, lists of goods not eligible for purchase, prohibitions on retransfer, and limits on both replacement of the goods and their use except in national defense. Accords of this sort would begin to facilitate a reconciliation of the commercial interests of the sellers, the needs of the recipients, and certain aims of conventional arms control. Overall levels of international transactions might not be affected, and recipients would still have access to systems needed for legitimate security purposes. However, the ultimate disposition and employment of purchased arms could be more strictly controlled.

The bilateral approach is certainly most interesting in cases in which long-term ties exist or are being created between a large producer and a large recipient, such as between the United States and Iran or Saudi Arabia. Each party can learn what the other's wants and intentions are, and third parties can see more clearly the limits and implications of a bilateral arms relationship of concern to them. The bilateral approach may be best for those situations almost totally resistant to regional attempts at regulation—regions in which a potentially dominant state (such as Brazil or Iran) is committed to a major arms acquisition program in order to build its power and exert greater influence in the region. In this sort of situation, there is little hope for a regional approach but perhaps some hope for a bilateral approach.

The bilateral approach would seem particularly sensible for the Persian Gulf. On one side, there is considerable capacity to buy on the part of a few oil states; on the other, there are many arms-producing states that need to balance their oil-import costs with an increase in arms exports to the region. Moreover, the exporters are interested in establishing broader and deeper relationships with the big oil states in hopes of cultivating strategically important friendships and securing oil supplies at decent prices. And the key importers, conservative states that are acutely concerned about long-term Soviet aims in their areas, have a strong strategic interest in special relationships with the United States and secure, if restricted, access to arms supplies. Thus, special bonds between the two categories of states could permit control of arms transfers.

The *regional approach* to limiting arms imports of the Third World has the best prospects for the future for the one essential reason that the proliferation of conventional weapons is closely linked to elements of regional security. The remainder of this essay deals with variations of this approach.

TWO

The Regional Approach
to Arms-Import Restraint

REGIONAL ASPECTS OF THE DEMAND FOR ARMS

Regional security objectives and concerns feed the demand for conventional arms in the Third World. Conversely, the infusion of conventional arms into a region can create or aggravate tensions and increase the likelihood and severity of hostilities. Furthermore, prospects for building a consensus on the need for arms control efforts should be greater at the regional than the global level. Finally, only at the regional level is there a high possibility of designing arms restraint that is sensitive to the legitimate needs of all the participants and the overall objective of balanced power.

The need for weapons can be explained by internal, international, and local or regional factors. The internal factors are well known: the desire of a regime for prestige and popular support, the need for internal security against rebellious forces within, and the need to satisfy the military-bureaucratic complex that props up—or could threaten—the political regime. The international factors are equally well known: the commercial, political, and military advisory pressures exerted by the large producer states to generate demand among the recipients; reduced confidence among client states that their one-time protectors have the means and sustained will to provide protection; and the consequent greater interest among the clients in providing for their own security with large quantities of sophisticated arms available from the protectors and others. But regional factors, too often over-looked, are of paramount importance, especially in the Third World.

There is an obvious relationship between the existence of regional conflict and the sustained desire of the regional states—not just those directly involved in conflict—to acquire new weapons, to replenish stockpiles, and to improve their combat skills and readiness. In the Middle East, in the Indian subconti-nent, in the Aegean, and in Southeast Asia—all highly conflictual over the last decade or so—there is little evidence that demand will abate in the 1980s. Southern Africa and the Maghreb both appear to be en route to greater violence, and arms transfers are increasing accordingly.

In the absence of open conflict, the maintenance of a regional balance of politico-military power will largely decide the demand for arms. Where all states in a region accept the principle of balance, the demand for arms can be kept low, though there will be some flow due to hedging against future instability among the regional states. This has been the situation in Latin America up to now. By contrast, if an important regional actor eschews its commitment to equilibrium, or if its neighbors suspect it of doing so, the race to acquire arms may begin. That could become the situation in the Persian Gulf in relations between Iran and the Emirates; in the Maghreb if Morocco or Algeria seeks to achieve a position of superior strength; in Latin America if Brazilian ambitions or power exceed the limits of balance; in black Africa if Nigeria becomes increasingly assertive vis-à-vis her weaker, poorer neighbors.

Chronic regional conflict, regional balances of power, the emergence of regional hegemones or claimants—these are the regional security parameters that will determine how most Third World states define their arms needs in the next decade. General international security issues will be of less concern to most developing countries than in the days when no state, however small and remote, could escape the geostrategic competition between East and West. And internal factors can explain only what might be called the "normal" demand for arms, that is, enough arms to placate a few generals and pacify the countryside.

So the primary sources of "excessive" demand for arms by Third World states are to be found in regional security patterns. And since the first aim of arms control—in this case, import restraint—must be to curb excessive demand while allowing for normal needs, a regional focus is critical.

Arms transfers will of course affect as well as be affected by regional security conditions. They will provide the means for regional destabilization, which will in turn engender a process of mistrust and perceived threat that will accelerate arms acquisitions throughout the region. The volume, quality, and distribution of incoming arms will largely determine the risks and costs facing a state that has an interest in revising the status quo. Arms imports might also impede regional progress toward the establishment of norms and institutions designed for conflict prevention and resolution, thus contributing indirectly to security problems in the long run.[4]

There are three levels in the process of regional arms acquisition: *initiation, escalation*, and *saturation*. At any moment in a given region, of course, one or more states may be farther up the ladder than the rest of the region. The Persian Gulf, for example, is now generally at the initiation level in arms acquisitions, though Iran and Saudi Arabia are already well into the escalation phase. In contrast, the Middle East and the Indian subcontinent have reached a level of saturation, in which arms replacement (more or less one-for-one) is now the dominant pattern. Southern Africa is at the initiation level, but with a few states (South Africa, Zaire) already in the escalatory phase.

From the point of view of instituting restraint, it is important to estimate the level of each region. The attitudes of states, and therefore the opportunities and techniques for regulating their demand for arms, will vary greatly depending on whether the states are just beginning to acquire weapons, or have already achieved a high level of armaments, and on whether all states in the region are at the same level of militarization.

[4]It might also be that in some instances arms imports, insofar as they enhance stability, might foster regional conflict-management efforts. But in general, a stable region with low arms levels would be better able to establish security institutions than a stable region with high arms levels.

Processes of Arms Acquisition

The normal procedure by which Third World states seek to satisfy their demand for arms is direct acquisition, through aid or purchase, from the main producer countries. It is clear that the development of new weapons systems (in particular, precision-guided munitions) and the modernization of classical weapons systems (such as fighter and attack aircraft) will continue in the key producer states and that few states of the Third World will have the alternative of national production of the most advanced weaponry. Where national production is pursued, its limits will be quickly reached. Capital costs, insufficient scale, and technological-managerial handicaps will prevent any profound market transformation in the next decade as long as the key producer states are willing to export plenty of their latest systems. Developing states will continue to rely mainly on large transactions in sophisticated armaments with industrialized countries.

This will not prevent the development of what could be called "regional markets" in the Third World. Small- and medium-size producers will emerge, perhaps capable of satisfying some regional demand for certain types of weapons. Intraregional (Iran–Jordan, Saudi Arabia–Egypt) as well as interregional transfers (Pakistan–Middle East, Israel–Latin America) could develop. We are now witnessing the development of an arms industry in the Arab world and the Persian Gulf,[5] and one can imagine competition in the Arab market of the 1980s among Iran, Egypt, and Saudi Arabia. India, Brazil, South Africa, and Israel are all moving toward sufficiently large-scale production of heavy weapons to permit significant exports. There will also be regional "stockpilers" (e.g., Vietnam) and regional "agitators" (e.g., Libya and Angola) with both new and used arms in excess of national needs at their disposal, capable of meeting some regional demand should the major producers hold back. Recipients will include subnational groups as well as states.

Finally, co-production and subcontracting between industrial producers and Third World producers are very likely to grow

[5]The creation of the Organization for Arab Arms Industry (AMIO), including Egypt, Saudi Arabia, Qatar, and the United Arab Emirates.

steadily in the next decade. These arrangements include construction under license, joint bilateral financing of weapons construction, and joint production. It will not be unusual for certain importer states to become co-producers or subcontractees and ultimately, having acquired the requisite skills and capacity, exporters of conventional arms. This pattern is being followed by Israel, South Africa, Pakistan, Iran, and Brazil. Co-production and subcontracting could exacerbate the competitive accumulation of conventional arms in various regions. Once co-production is established with one state in a region, others will want to engage in similar arrangements to ensure against eventual local power imbalance due to differential indigenous production capabilities. The industrialized states will no doubt be very accommodating toward this demand.

In sum, just as regional security conditions will critically affect and be affected by the demand for conventional arms, the regional dimension of arms trade will grow in importance in the 1980s. If the demand for arms in the Third World can be explained primarily by regional factors, then regional action will be most fruitful in containing this demand.

REGIONAL ASPECTS OF ARMS CONTROL

Under what conditions can regional arms control agreements be effective and durable? As indicated above, the demand for arms is directly linked to the general perception of regional security and to the particular interests and fears of the states involved. Agreed restrictions on arms imports will be impossible unless and until the behavior of and relations among states of a region rise above a minimum threshold of mutual confidence. This is not to say that arms control is possible only when it is no longer needed, that is, when all serious regional security problems have been overcome. Arms restraint may be possible well before a region is pacified and may contribute significantly to the institutionalization and bureaucratization of conditions and habits of normalization.

The so-called Six Johnson Principles presented by former U.S. President Lyndon Johnson at the United Nations Conference of the Committee on Disarmament in April 1966 are useful in identifying a set of guiding principles for realizing arms control measures:

- The first and most obvious principle is that there can be no effective arms control unless the countries involved are seriously interested in mutual restraint (rather than harboring ulterior motives).

- Second, the initiative should normally come from within the region concerned; generally, international bodies and other outside parties can only encourage and facilitate the initiatives stemming from among the interested parties.

- Third, an arrangement regulating the demand for arms must not exclude any country of the region capable of disrupting the arrangements through general disruptive behavior or, in particular, by a sustained high level of arms imports.

- Fourth, external suppliers must agree to respect the regional arrangement, thus enhancing its international stature and reducing the danger that outside pressures or circumvention would spoil the effort.

- Fifth, the arrangements must contribute to the maintenance of a stable military balance. The control measures should not impair the security of any state in the region, for the remedy would then be worse than the illness.

- Sixth—a principle that cuts through the others—the interests of all the parties must be respected. This is the principle of initial and sustained consensus, essential to the effectiveness of the adopted measures.[6]

Political Preconditions

Translating these principles into political preconditions, they can be summarized under three headings: initiative, consensus, and maturity. A determined initiative, capable of gaining at least the

[6]The "Six Johnson Principles" have been frequently reiterated in American proposals on regulating arms trade, most recently by Ambassador J. Martin before the Conference on the Committee on Disarmament (CCD), April 10, 1975 (Doc. CCD/PV665).

interest, if not the immediate endorsement, of other states of the region, is obviously necessary. Preferably, such an initiative would originate within the region, either from one or several states (such as the Peruvian initiative in Latin America that preceded the Declaration of Ayacucho) or from a regional organization [such as the Organization of African Unity (OAU), the Arab League, or the Association of Southeat Asian Nations (ASEAN)]. Where regional insecurity and distrust are not acute, a process inspired from within will stand more chance of acceptance than one pressed upon the parties from the outside. But the impulse will have to come from outside if no state in the region is willing to take the initiative (perhaps for fear of appearing weak) or if any initiative taken by one of the states is automatically dismissed or suspected by its neighbors. Finally, the initiative can be mixed: joint action by a state or institution of the region and some external states or organization.

The second political precondition is the formation of regional consensus on arms control goals. The refusal to participate by any one important state will preclude an agreement or lead to its eventual unraveling, unless the aloof state conforms in deed to what it refuses to accept on record. It is impossible to conceive of meaningful arms restraint throughout South America not involving Brazil, and equally impossible to conceive of it in the Persian Gulf without Iran. If the region is still at the "initiation" level of arms acquisition, the consensus must be based on the goals of preventing arms imports and limiting internal production. If the region is in the "escalation" phase, the consensus should be on freezing the existing levels, perhaps with some allowances to achieve balance. If the region has reached the "saturation" level, the consensus should be on reducing existing arsenals without prejudice to regional balance or the security of any given state.

The third political precondition is sufficient regional political maturity to translate consensus on goals into durable practical implementation. If the technical measures envisaged for restricting imports are designed genuinely to arrest or reduce arms levels, the participating states must be willing to live with limits on and intrusions (in the form of exchanges of information, verification measures, etc.) into their sovereignty. Thus, beyond the immediate consensus on arms-restraint goals, a minimal regional sociopolitical understanding (though not necessarily what one would call "community") will be necessary for states to engage successfully in the required extension of confidence and trust. This maturity may have existed for a long time (Latin America) or may develop quite rapidly in a previously chaotic region (the Middle East or black Africa in the 1980s). In some regions this condition will be manifested in existing organizations—as in Latin America [Organization of American States (OAS)], black Africa (OAU), and the Arab world (Arab League).

These conditions obviously cannot all be satisfied in all regions, at least in the next decade, which leads us to the problem of appraising the present and future nature of different regions of the Third World.

Regional Indicators

Some regions will be more or less "ripe" for arms control, and so an initiative would have chances of success. In others, the three preconditions will not be satisfied. It is impossible to predict with confidence which regions will be ready when. Moreover, there is no determinism in this process: an initiative and subsequent success in restraining arms will not necessarily sprout whenever the preconditions have been satisfied. But we can devise some regional indicators to help see what regions are more predisposed than others to the implementation of regional import restraint and how such measures must vary from region to region in order to be effective. There are three important regional indicators: the presence or absence of regional *conflict*, the presence or absence of regional power *equilibrium*, and the presence or absence of regional *cooperation*.

1. Conflict—armed or unarmed, interstate or intrastate—within a region does not necessarily preclude the establishment of a system of arms-import controls. To be sure, conflict fans the demand for arms, and the prevalence of conflictual relationships makes difficult any initiative toward limiting demand. But the attitudes of states vis-à-vis conflict itself must be considered along with their attitudes toward one another.

Fatigue over chronic conflict or trauma from a recent experience in acute regional violence can alter regional attitudes. Emphasis may shift from strategic competition to internal development as a means of national elevation, especially if the latter has suffered due to the former pursuit (as seems to have been the case in the Middle East). Taking this perspective—above all, if there is a saturation of arms—one might find circumstances favorable for the establishment of a certain type of regional arms control. We will examine below what model of arms control can be envisaged in such circumstances.

2. Regional equilibrium is a key factor in the success of any arms restraint effort since it permits states to agree more easily on limitation measures without any state feeling that its security will be immediately impaired. In contrast, the persistence or appearance of disequilibrium or hegemony—or lingering suspicions that not all states would resist such temptations—would preclude anything more than ephemeral initiatives toward restraint. This difficulty is compounded where asymmetries exist in the potential for indigenous production among the states in the region. As suggested earlier, where a region is out of equilibrium, a bilateral approach (such as contract stipulations restricting the volume and sorts of arms going to a regional power), or an agreement worked out among exporters not to contribute to regional instability, would be more likely to succeed than regional recipient restraint.

3. The potential for or existence of cooperation among the states of a region may stem from increasingly close functional interaction (trade, transportation, etc.) or from a measure of social integration. Normally, a high degree of socialization and interaction is translated into at least incipient institutionalization through regional organizations of a broad (such as the OAU, or the OAS) or narrow (technical agencies, joint use of waterways, etc.) character. While the existence of a regional organization is not in itself evidence of sufficient regional cooperation to support an arms restraint effort, some cooperative experience would obviously help. With respect to arms control, the opening of states to one another for exchange of

information and views both requires and can contribute to the mutual trust and understanding that is essential if the states are to accept limitations on their means of protecting themselves from their neighbors.

The character of a region will determine whether and how the political preconditions mentioned earlier can best be satisfied. The diversity of regional situations and trends suggests the need for diverse models of regional arms control. All regions cannot be subject to a regional arms control process. But neither must all regions perfectly fit a single model that depends on what might intuitively seem to be optimal conditions for progress in achieving restraint.

THREE

Models for Regional Arms Control and for Limitations on Arms Demand

One might identify three basic models for regional arms control, corresponding to three distinguishable types of situations: the Tlatelolco, Sinai, and Vienna models. Though they all require the coincidence of an initiative, consensus on goals, and sociopolitical maturity, each assumes different regional political conditions and a specific type of arms race. Each has different goals and employs different techniques.

THE TLATELOLCO MODEL[7]

Conventional arms limitation in this case aims at *preventing* an arms race in an area with some experience in regional cooperation. The region is still at the initiation point of the armament process. Although large orders may be in the process of being filled, or expectations of arms escalation may abound, the level of conventional arms is still low. Tranquility and power equilibrium have historically characterized the area. The three political preconditions would seem readily attainable: an initiative is feasible on the part of any number of states; forming consensus should not founder on insurmountable problems; regional maturity exists.

Conditions in this type of region are propitious for the implementation of a fairly elaborate and effective form of arms

[7]So named because of its general similarity to the Latin American effort (the Treaty of Tlatelolco) to keep *nuclear* weapons out of Latin America.

control. The region is peaceful and cooperative enough for the region's states to take seriously an initiative by one of their ranks aimed at preventing rising armament levels. The basic goal on which consensus is to form must be that of limiting arms imports from outside the region. Regional security and stability are rarely enhanced by a general rise in arms levels, especially in a region with a history of tranquility. It is in the interest of the states of a region to maintain a balance of power at a low level, not only to avoid massive expenditures without improved security, but in fact to reduce the dangers of disequilibrium. For example, at low regional arms levels, Brazil is merely the biggest, richest Latin American state. At high levels, given Brazil's ability to acquire more arms more quickly than its neighbors, regional stability could seriously suffer.

Given the rather favorable regional security conditions, rules should be established relating to imports of certain categories of weapons unnecessary for national defense (heavy battle tanks, fighter bombers, amphibious vehicles, and missiles). It seems more crucial to limit the introduction of these types of arms than to set a ceiling on total weapons levels, for it is more important to prevent the creation of offensive capabilities in normally peaceful regions where there is no justification for such capabilities. Therefore, *qualitative limits* on arms imports are of top priority.

Direct action on specified imports should be accompanied by the initiation of exchanges of information and views concerning *all* activities related to arms acquisition. These exchanges, designed to reinforce mutual confidence, would include national statistics on arms production and imports, information on defense budgets, advance notification of all arms purchases (even those falling within established limits), and publicizing of all co-production and subcontracting ventures. Going beyond this, the process might involve a requirement that a justification for all acquisitions be registered with a central regional arms monitoring agency and reviewed by the other participants.

The second step in the Tlatelolco approach would be directed toward regulating national production and co-production. If the present danger is an escalation in arms levels through imports, the future danger—perhaps sharpened by imports restraint—is an escalation through indigenous production or co-production by a regional state with an external state. Regulating imports alone would, in the long run, be ineffective and discriminatory. The second step must be attained if the whole edifice is not eventually to collapse or become obsolete. There are various possible approaches to this second step: development of a regulated regional arms market, controlling regional production of various systems, or regional co-production.

Should such a process be formal or informal? The character of the region and of the objectives makes the establishment of *formal* rules, written into a regional treaty, both possible and desirable. Such a treaty—a "conventional Tlatelolco"—would establish precise rules banning or limiting acquisitions of certain arms. The accord should contain protocols open to outside arms-producing states willing to bind themselves to the regional limits on military sales and grants. The commitment of outsiders to respect the treaty would provide an added layer of protection in the event of abrogation by one of the regional signatories. The agreement should have provisions for periodic review and, if necessary, amendment to keep pace with advances in weapons technology. Finally, such a treaty must contain verification and enforcement provisions. The nature of enforcement will depend on the sociopolitical maturity of the region, the degree of confidence among the states that they will not find themselves in or near violation, and the competence of regional agencies established. Enforcement measures might range from collective intraregional economic or diplomatic sanctions to the imposition of arms embargoes by external signatories.

Normally, the preexistence of a regional political-security organization would facilitate control-through-publicity, information sharing, and dispute resolution. An established institution could also carry out verification procedures, using regional inspectors and auditors to monitor compliance with the treaty by comparing acquired data with commitments and statements made by the states regarding imports (as is done in controlling international narcotics traffic), and, later, with commitments to restrain indigenous arms production [as done by the International Atomic Energy Agency (IAEA) with regard to the nuclear industry].

The control agency would contain representatives of all contracting states; its secretariat would have the authority to conclude agreements with international organizations and extraregional arms exporters.

In the absence of extant regional political-security institutions (such absence being unlikely in this model, since most regions that meet the model's requirements would probably have at least incipient institutions), a special monitoring and administering agency would have to be created. Even if an established regional institution existed, an arms control agency might be more effective if kept autonomous, given the specificity of its tasks and the need for consistent performance irrespective of the vicissitudes of regional politics. In fact, most existing regional organizations are not well suited to functioning as technical arms control agents. Either they are alliances rather than security organizations (such as the Arab League) or their institutional development remains embryonic (such as the ASEAN). These organizations would find it very difficult to fulfill these new arms-restraint functions. A special agency, created by treaty, financed by the states party to it, and linked to the existing regional organization, might be more productive.

At the same time, the role of the larger regional organization remains essential to the general promotion of regional security. The assemblies and councils of the central body could serve as a permanent forum for identifying threats to regional peace, conflict resolution, political consultation, and enforcement. This function would be closely linked to the technical functions of the control agency. There must be a combination of *technical measures* to implement arms restraint and *political measures* to strengthen regional security. The Tlatelolco model might thus involve two distinct but linked institutional structures.

Considering regional trends and characteristics, the Tlatelolco model would seem to have a reasonable chance of success if applied to Latin America, black Africa, and the Maghreb in the 1980s.

Latin America is the most fertile region for such an enterprise. The Declaration of Ayacucho of December 1974, made by eight governments of the region,[8] created a favorable climate. The initiative of Peru in January 1974, in proposing a 10-year moratorium on imports of major weapons systems by the Andean countries, was the real trigger for the whole enterprise. The main goal of Ayacucho is the creation of mechanisms among the states of the Andean group to halt the acquisition of offensive weapons and to eliminate "excessive expenditures" on arms in general. Since the declaration there have been several gatherings of the Andean Pact countries aimed at putting the terms of the declaration into effect. Most nonaligned countries and the United States have supported the declaration. Yet there has been virtually no progress beyond the declaratory stage. Most of the signatories have gone on to procure high-performance aircraft. The initiator, Peru, has shown an appetitite for arms imports second to none among the group.

The existing institutional base—regional and subregional—for this enterprise is impressive: the OAS, the Andean Pact, the Latin American Economic Commission. This said, however, it should be noted that there is no automatic connection between institutional experience and regional arms restraint. The sovereignty and security of states are potentially too profoundly affected for meaningful arms control to be a simple extension of existing political cooperation.

Significantly, Brazil has been very hesitant vis-à-vis the whole enterprise and is well into the escalation phase of national arms acquisition. If Brazil should strive for regional hegemony or engage any of its neighbors in a hostile fashion, Latin America would no longer be so amenable to the establishment of an effective system of regional arms-import restraint. The situation would be comparable to that of the Persian Gulf, and a bilateral approach to arms restraint—with the United States, Brazil's principal supplier, actively involved—would hold greater promise.

Likewise, if conflictual trends maintain their momentum in Africa, application of the Tlatelolco model might also be impossi-

[8]Argentina, Bolivia, Chile, Colombia, Ecuador, Panama, Peru, and Venezuela.

ble there. The present equipping of Zaire by the United States and France, the aftereffects of the Angola affair, and the prospect of violent political transformation in Southern Africa are all disturbing developments. Now at the initiation stage, an escalation of arms may be in store, with the acquisition of Soviet arms by Congo-Brazzaville, the Sudan, Uganda, Tanzania, and above all Angola, in response to, but also stimulating, arms acquisitions from the West by South Africa, Nigeria, Kenya, and Zaire. None of these arms flows is of the magnitude of those going to the Persian Gulf. But the appearance of a process of escalation could, in a few years' time, upset regional equilibrium in black Africa, undo the glacial progress toward cooperation through the OAU, and foreclose the possibilities of an African Tlatelolco in conventional arms. Although present political conditions in black Africa are hardly ideal for an initiative to be launched and to gather consensus on arms import restraint, conditions may be worse several years from now.

One could reason similarly with regard to the Maghreb. This region could satisfy the political preconditions for arms control in a few years. Or, because of a rise in Algerian and Moroccan power or vicious competition between them, the area could become a field of confrontation totally unsuited to the model just outlined. Each of the three regions can be the subject of several scenarios, depending on the evolution of regional power configurations and, of course, on whether or not regional arms-import restraint is tried and succeeds. But the Tlatelolco model can be applied only in the best of conditions: the region must be peaceful, in equilibrium, cooperative, and still "unspoiled" by an excessive arms race.

THE SINAI MODEL

Conventional arms control—and, specifically, regional import restraint—is also possible in a conflict-ridden region already saturated with sophisticated offensive and defensive weapons, in which social integration and functional cooperation are nil and mistrust and conflict are long-standing. Paradoxically, all the political preconditions for instituting regional restraint may still be present, though a totally different arms control model is required. Where can the initiative, the consensus, the maturity originate in this case?

In fact, it is the very saturation of arms and the exhausting permanence of conflict that can, brutally but logically, bring about the needed structural and attitudinal conditions. The leaders of the region will have good reason to conclude that maintaining totally conflictual relations can only prevent the satisfaction of many important but neglected national objectives. With all parties well armed and yet none in a position to press further toward hegemony, a degree of equilibrium exists. Out of the permanent conflict, and with the passing of old warriors, may arise an impulse—long suppressed—to pacify intraregional relations and achieve a certain regional maturity.

In this perspective, the primary goal around which consensus must form is not the limiting of the demand for arms per se but the progressive establishment of a security system involving political, economic, and arms control elements. Arms restraint is but one of the elements in this general approach. The hope is not to demilitarize and integrate the region but to avert a future as violent as the past. We call this the "Sinai model" because the Sinai agreement reached between Egypt and Israel in 1975 can be considered a sort of prefiguration.

The first step may be the most difficult, given the towering hurdle of venomous distrust. An outside initiative will normally be required: the poor quality of regional politics and the sensitivity of domestic politics in each state make an initiative from within difficult, even if the leaders are privately interested in changing course. Only an outside initiative will enable the states of the region to lower their guard a bit. Such an external initiative might be stimulated by the perception of one or more outside powers that their interests are in jeopardy because of the region's chronic conflict, or the first step might be taken by an organ of the UN.

What process should follow the initiative? Most important is the passage from a state of conflict to one of minimally normalized relations. The goal is political; arms control is an auxiliary measure, a mechanism both to help institutionalize and to encourage further political relaxation. Conventional arms will have played too central a role in regional relations to be omitted from the normalization process. Further arms acquisitions would reflect a desire to arrest the process, or at least would lead to that perception. Reduced imports, followed by reduced overall levels, would indicate the opposite.

This is a totally different process than that of the Tlatelolco model, in which the prime objective is the prevention of arms escalation that might cause a region to become increasingly conflict-ridden. In the case of the Sinai model, the first substantive step is political—a truce, a cease-fire, an armistice, an international conference or mediation—followed by more functional efforts to reduce insecurity: exchanges of information on troop movements, implacement of international observers, limits on troop deployments, territorial neutralizations, frontier demilitarization, and measures to enforce the decisions agreed upon. The gradual accumulation of rules in the initial absence of—but contributing toward—mutual confidence among the states will require sustained external pressure, possibly having to take the form of security guarantees.

Within this inchoate security system, measures affecting armaments might take two forms: reciprocal information exchanges on arms acquisitions and *quantitative* restrictions or ceilings on imports. Hostile states may resist normalization unless they have faith in their own national defense forces. It will therefore be difficult, if not unwise, to touch their arsenals in any significant and immediate way. But it should be possible to reconcile the needs for security with restraint on the growth of overall capabilities that may be considered normal for a region fraught with conflict but excessive in a region moving toward normalization. Quantitative ceilings would constitute a first knot in the strangulation of arms imports. The gradual normalization of regional relations will require increasingly forthcoming negotiations, eventually dealing with restrictions on particular weapons categories and with more general quantitative reductions.

One can conceive of a general treaty on normalizing relations that would have annexes pertaining to arms. Afterward, a permanent negotiating forum would have to be created so that the states of the region would have a place to discuss proposals and gradually adopt measures strengthening their security. An armistice commission or an ad hoc committee could serve as the preliminary forum for this process.

Key arms-exporting states should also participate in these forums so that they can act in full conformity with the rules laid down. In fact, the whole enterprise will be impossible without agreement by the producers. If they maintain dynamic, competitive export strategies vis-à-vis the region, based on commercial incentives or geostrategic ambitions, regional recipient restraint will be difficult to sustain. The participation of the producers can be formal or informal, but external commitments to respect the regional effort are crucial. Verification of arms-restraint measures should involve states from both inside and outside the region, so that it will permit a sense of local participation but not be frustrated at the first regional crisis.

In what regions of the world might such a model apply in the 1980s? The Middle East, the Indian subcontinent, and the Korean peninsula are all likely to be conflict-ridden regions, saturated with armaments, that might sooner or later become exhausted with their conflicts. In the Middle East, the initiative and the consensus for arms restraint might result from a combination of external action—especially United States policy—and the modification of the attitudes of certain key states of the region, Egypt in particular.

With regard to the Indian subcontinent, there are three problems that might militate against application of the Sinai model. First, as long as India and Pakistan are deeply suspicious of each other's intentions, any initiative taken within the region would probably be interpreted as yet another machination; therefore, the initiative would have to come from outside the region. But no outside actor is so vitally interested in pacifying the Indian subcontinent as to undertake a determined initiative of possible interest to the key regional actors. (In contrast, the stakes in the Middle East are so high for outside powers that one might have higher hopes that one or more of those powers would launch an arms control initiative there, just as the United States has taken a diplomatic initiative.) Second, the close link between the posture of Iran and the security of both India and Pakistan causes an overlap between two distinct regions that is problematic for arms control. How can arms limitations between India and Pakistan be implemented without taking into account Iran's policy of military build-up and the new possible disequilibria on the region's periphery? Finally, India's domestic production potential is so much greater than that of Pakistan that the latter would almost certainly not accept limits on arms imports without credible assurances that indigenous production would also be controlled.

As far as Korea is concerned, intraregional relations remain highly conflictual and tense. It is hard to see a modification of attitudes springing from within the region. External pressure is possible, but might have only limited effect. If arms transfer restraint is to come to Korea, it will almost certainly have to be negotiated and imposed by the United States and the Soviet Union.

THE VIENNA MODEL[9]

Conventional arms limitation can, finally, entail reducing the level of armaments in a region that is saturated with weapons and haunted by hostility but that also has some experience in cooperation, at least enough that the actors can appreciate that their hostility does not require the maintenance of such high force levels. Because the region is saturated with arms, it might be possible to negotiate reductions without any effect on the security of the states. If the conflictual history accounts for the regional overarmament, the attenuation of conflict should alter attitudes toward arms levels in general and imports in particular. The first step of the Vienna model would involve an initiative on the part of the states of the region, acting either individually or collectively. A negotiation regarding both quantitative and qualitative arms reductions and the establishment of confidence-building measures (e.g., advance notice of maneuvers) must follow. The logic

[9]So named because it is generally patterned after the approach to mutual force reductions in Europe currently under negotiation in Vienna.

of such a combination of measures is that it can simultaneously reduce tensions that encourage high force levels while also reducing existing military capabilities themselves.

Qualitative reductions would be aimed at the withdrawal from the region or the destruction of numbers of particularly destabilizing weapons systems (tanks, attack aircraft, surface-to-surface missiles). But freedom to modernize forces would be unimpaired by mere quantitative restrictions. In fact, quantitative force reductions might spur states to improve the quality of their forces in order to maintain the same combat potential at lower levels.

Still, quantitative reductions would contribute significantly to public awareness of and support for relaxation. But they should be carefully designed so as not to cut national defenses beneath a threshold consistent with the maintenance of stability and public confidence in security. Quantitative reductions should proceed on the basis of the establishment of ceilings, either equal or differential, regional or subregional. These ceilings could apply to a specific zone constituting the most sensitive heartland of the region or to all states participating in the negotiation.

Such careful quantitative reductions might be hard to achieve and should not be allowed to impede progress in *qualitative* restrictions. Perhaps the best course would be as follows: first to set quantitative ceilings; then to establish qualitative restrictions constraining certain types of existing weapons (as through prohibitions on replacement or modernization or through ceilings on specific weapons) while regulating the deployment of new weapons within particularly sensitive zones; then to work out institutional arrangements covering information sharing on military budgets, force deployments, research and development, etc.; finally to conduct further efforts at making deeper quantitative cuts.

The Vienna model would be applicable in regions characterized by a coexistence of conflict and cooperation. This mixed quality indicates a need for true negotiations, and not simply harmonious deliberations among socially integrated states. Thus, certain elements of the Sinai model would be required; in particular, a permanent forum would have to be created whose agenda and level of activity would vary but which, once formed, could not be dissolved even if the negotiations were to drag on interminably or be disrupted by a flare-up of regional tensions.

In what regions can the Vienna model be applied? It is of course already being attempted in Europe, though in a most desultory way. The European continent is an overarmed region, yet it continues to absorb great quantities of the most advanced conventional weapons. But the acquisition of these arms is occurring in a unique context. The cold war produced the political, ideological, and military division of the European continent, and it created two antagonistic military organizations grouping the majority of the states around one or the other global superpower.

No conflict has been unleashed between these two military organizations for 30 years now. The tension of the 1950s has abated substantially; new relationships between the member states of the two alliances have made general war on the European continent less likely. There is an uncertain equilibrium of conventional forces, but nuclear deterrence constitutes the essential element of security and stability.

The conventional weaponry currently deployed in Europe as well as new acquisitions of precision-guided weapons and new generations of tanks and aircraft do not pose problems of the same order as those posed by the militarization of the Persian Gulf or Southern Africa. However, it may be that the evolution of forces in Europe, the new conventional deployments of the two pacts, and the prospects for a "decoupling" of American deterrence in Europe, will transform the European situation and increase the risk of limited conventional conflict on the continent. The processes for conventional arms control in Europe—in particular, the Mutual Force Reduction (MFR) negotiations—should be evaluated not only in the light of existing conditions but also in the context of plausible alternative futures for Europe. The Vienna model will succeed in Europe only if cooperation prevails over confrontation. A cooperative Europe, at peace and in equilibrium—even if it remains divided into distinct, opposing systems—will satisfy the political preconditions. The tasks for Europe are to remain peaceful, maintain a stable balance, and expand cooperative links.

The Vienna model could also be applied to regions where the

Sinai model has already been implemented. The attainment of a freeze on arms in a region saturated with arms and exhausted by ancient conflict can evolve toward the Vienna model as long as momentum persists. In this sense, the Middle East may become a region conducive to the application of the Vienna model.

While the obstacles to its implementation might be as great as those for the Sinai model, the Vienna model might also be applied in the Indian subcontinent, a region already well stocked with arms and, one would hope, finished with episodic hostilities. But the cautious experiments with normalization in the last five years hardly represent a cooperative experience comparable to détente, *ostpolitik*, the Conference on Security and Cooperation in Europe, and MFR. Furthermore, the territorial status quo in the region has not been fully accepted by all the states of the region, and India's apparent hegemonic aspirations and potential could cause serious future instability. But there is a chance that the Indian subcontinent will be ready for negotiated arms restraint along the lines of the Vienna model by the end of the next decade.

RECAPITULATION

The following tables summarize the important factors in determining the applicability of each regional arms control model:

Political Preconditions	Arms Level	Regional Indicators	
Initiative	Initiation	Conflictual	Peaceful
Consensus	Escalation	Disequilibrated	Equilibrated
Sociopolitical maturity	Saturation	Uncooperative	Integrated

Any effort to regulate international traffic in conventional arms must deal not only with production and exports but also with demand itself. Because of the historical, political, and military diversity of the international system, regulating the demand for

195

Regions Conducive to Arms Control

Region Type and Indicators	Arms Level	Goal	Possible Regions
1			
Peaceful Equilibrated Cooperative	Initiation	Nonarmament	Latin America Black Africa Maghreb
2			
Conflictual Equilibrated Uncooperative	Saturation	Establishment of security systems	Middle East Indian subcontinent Korea
3			
Semiconflictual Equilibrated Semicooperative	Saturation	Reductions	Europe Indian subcontinent Middle East after successful application of Sinai model
4			
Peaceful Disequilibrated Uncooperative	Escalation	Qualitative restrictions	Persian Gulf
5			
Conflictual Disequilibrated Uncooperative	Initiation/ escalation	Nonarmament	Southern Africa

arms cannot take the same form everywhere. Controls are possible only if adapted to specific regional situations. Pragmatism and relativism are essential. But while it is possible for regional groupings to take serious initiatives and develop effective restraint on their own, the broader international community must show a new attitude toward conventional arms control. A general change in climate is needed to foster initiatives among recipients; external actors can provide encouragement, example, and a commitment to respect organized efforts among recipients.

Applicability of the Three Regional Models

Model	Process		Region Type
Tlatelolco	Initiative:	internal	1
	First stage:	*qualitative* limits on imports, confidence-building measures, ad hoc technical enforcement organs, rules applied to external producers	
	Second stage:	limits on indigenous production, controls on co-production	
Sinai	Initiative:	internal-external coordinated	2
	First stage:	general security agreement, including commitment to arms control, *quantitative* limits on imports, rules applied to external producers, permanent forums for negotiations	
	Second stage:	reduction of arms levels	
Vienna	Initiative:	internal	3
	First stage:	*quantitative* reductions and *qualitative* restrictions	
	Second stage:	limitations on budgets, research and development, etc.	

Selected Bibliography

"The Arms Business Must Be Curbed," *New York Times*, October 27, 1975, p. 38.

Arms Trade Registers: The Arms Trade with the Third World, Stockholm International Peace Research Institute, Almqvist and Wiksells, 1971.

Bader, William B.: "The Proliferation of Conventional Weapons," in Cyril E. Black, and Richard A. Falk: *The Future of the International Legal Order*, vol. III, *Conflict Management*, Princeton University Press, Princeton, N.J., 1971.

Cahn, Anne Hessing: "Arms Transfer Constraints: Why, Who, What, When and How," in Geoffrey Kemp (ed.), *The Military Build-up in Non-Industrial States*, forthcoming.

———: "Have Arms, Will Sell," *Arms Control Today,* vol. 4, no. 10, October 1974.

Callaghan, Thomas A., Jr.: *US/European Economic Cooperation in Military and Civil Technology*, Center for Strategic and International Studies, Georgetown University, Washington, D.C., 1975.

Controlling the Conventional Arms Race, United Nations Association–U.S.A, New York, 1976.

Culver, John: "Needed: A More Realistic and Informed Defense Debate," U.S. Congress, Senate, Press Release, March 1976.

The Economic Impact of Reductions in Defense Spending, U.S. Arms Control and Disarmament Agency, Washington, D.C., 1972.

Frank, Lewis A.: *The Arms Trade in International Relations*, Praeger Publishers, Inc., New York, 1969.

199

Gray, Colin S.: "Traffic Control for the Arms Trade?" *Foreign Policy,* no. 6, Spring 1972, pp. 153–169.

Harkavy, Robert: *The Arms Trade and International Systems,* Ballinger Publishing Co., Cambridge, Mass., 1975.

Holst, Johan J.: "What Is Really Going On?" *Foreign Policy,* no. 19, Summer 1975, pp. 155–163.

Kennedy, Edward M.: "The Persian Gulf: Arms Race or Arms Control?" *Foreign Affairs,* vol. 54, no. 1, October 1975.

Klare, Michael T.: "The Political Economy of Arms Sales," *Society,* September/October 1974.

Leiss, Amelia C., et. al.: *Arms Transferred to Less Developed Countries,* Center for International Studies, M.I.T., Cambridge, Mass., 1970.

————: *Changing Patterns of Arms Transfers: Implications for Arms Transfers Policies,* Pamphlet no. c/70–2, Massachusetts Institute of Technology, Cambridge, 1970.

Pranger, Robert J., and Dale R. Tahtinen: *Toward a Realistic Military Assistance Program,* American Enterprise Institute for Public Policy Research, Washington, D.C., 1974.

Rothschild, Emma: "The Boom in the Death Business," *The New York Review of Books,* October 2, 1975.

Sivard, Ruth Leger: *World Military and Social Expenditures, 1976,* W.M.S.E. Publications, Leesburg, Va., 1976.

Stanley, John, and Maurice Pearton: *The International Trade in Arms,* Praeger Publishers, Inc., New York, 1972.

World Military Expenditures and Arms Transfers, 1966–1975, U.S. Arms Control and Disarmament Agency, Washington, D.C., 1976.

Index

A-4 Skyhawk, transfers of, 33*n*.
Abu Dhabi, weapons acquisition by, 33, 35
ACDA (*see* United States Arms Control and Disarmament Agency)
Aerospatiale (Nord) MM-38 Exocet and Enta, transfers of, 33*n*.
Afghanistan, weapons acquisition by, 32
Africa, 79, 93, 118, 128, 174, 187
  Central, 146
  Horn of, 9
  Southern, 9, 17*n*., 117*n*., 128, 148, 174, 188, 194
    weapons acquisition by, 175, 196
  Sub-Saharan: weapons acquisition by, 144, 188
    weapons control by, 87, 153, 180, 186, 196
  West, 146
  (*See also specific countries*)
AID (Agency for International Development), 41
Air Defense Ground Environment, NATO, 73
Air-scatterable mines, 74
Aircraft carriers, 147
Algeria, 9*n*., 32, 174, 188
  conflict between Morocco and, 145
Allison, Graham T., 57*n*.
AMIO (Organization for Arab Arms Industry), 176*n*.
AMX-30, 116
Andean Pact (*see* Ayacucho Declaration)
Angola, 109, 117, 124, 127, 144
  weapons acquisition by, 128, 176, 188
Anti-aircraft weapons, 53
Antitank weapons, 53
Arab-Israeli War, 19, 31, 46, 52–54, 64, 70, 109, 126*n*., 129, 132, 144, 148, 165
  (*See also* Israel)

Arab League, 176, 179, 180, 186
Arab oil boycott, 122, 123
  (*See also* Organization of Petroleum Exporting Countries)
Arab Summit Conference (1974), 35
Area weapons, 55, 59–60, 100
Argentina, 32, 34, 78, 80–81, 98, 187*n*.
Arms acquisition, levels of, 175
Arms control approaches:
  bilateral, 23, 167, 169, 170
  collaborative, 20
  global, 20, 21, 167–169, 173
  multilateral, 20
  regional, 18, 19, 145, 147, 153, 167, 171–197
  unilateral, 23, 167–168
Arms control models:
  Sinai, 183, 188–193, 195, 197
  Tlatelolco, 183–188, 190
  Vienna, 183, 192–197
Arms embargo, 185
Arms Export Control Act (U.S.), 97
ASEAN (Association of Southeast Asian Nations), 179, 186
Asia, 164
  East, 6, 164
  South, 9, 10, 134, 146, 148, 191
    weapons acquisition by, 64, 175
    weapons control by, 19, 195, 196
  Southeast, 9, 17*n*., 118, 146, 174
    weapons acquisition by, 34, 79
    weapons control by, 195
  (*See also specific countries*)
Association of Southeast Asian Nations (ASEAN), 179, 186
At-1 "Snapper" and "Sagger," transfers of, 33*n*.
Australia, weapons production by, 119
Ayacucho Declaration (1974), 19*n*., 98, 179, 186–187

201

About the Authors

ANNE HESSING CAHN is currently Foreign Affairs officer at the U.S. Arms Control and Disarmament Agency. She has been a fellow at Harvard University's Program for Science and International Affairs and a research associate at the Center for International Studies, M.I.T. In 1971, she received her Ph.D. in political science from M.I.T., where she has also taught. Her many professional affiliations include Board of Directors, Arms Control Association; Board of Directors of SANE; Chairperson, Arms Control Committee, Forum on Physics and Society, American Physical Society. She is the author of numerous articles on arms control.

JOSEPH J. KRUZEL, who received his Ph.D. from Harvard, is assistant professor of political science at Duke University. His research interests include arms control and future causes of international conflict. He is the author of a forthcoming book on the history of arms control and has published articles in *Orbis, The Bulletin of Atomic Scientists, Armed Forces and Society,* and *Arms Control Today.* Professor Kruzel served for three years as a member of the United States delegation to the Strategic Arms Limitation Talks.

Colonel PETER M. DAWKINS is a professional Army officer currently serving as a troop commander at Fort Ord, California. During his eighteen years of commissioned service, Colonel Dawkins has had a full range of command and staff assignments both in the United States and overseas and has taught on the faculty at the U.S. Military Academy. In 1973, he was selected to be a White House Fellow, and served a tour as Military Assistant to the Deputy Secretary of Defense. Colonel Dawkins has a B.S. from West Point, a B.A. and M.A. from Oxford University, and an M.P.A. from Princeton University.

JACQUES HUNTZINGER is a professor at the University of Besançon and currently he is also a seminar director at the University of Paris I (Sorbonne) and at the École Nationale d'Administration in France. In addition to having contributed numerous articles to the newspapers *Le Monde* and the magazines *Nouvel Observateur, Politique Etrangère,* and *La Nouvelle Revue Socialiste,* Professor Huntzinger is a member of the Scientific Council of the Fondation d'Étude pour la Défense Nationale, and an associate of the Centre d'Étude de Politique Etrangère. He has a Doctor of Public Law, a Diploma from the Institute of Political Studies of Paris, and an Aggregation in Public Law degree.

DAVID C. GOMPERT contributed to this volume as a Senior Fellow of the 1980s Project at the Council on Foreign Relations, a position he held from 1975 until April 1977. He has since become Director of the Office of International Security Policy of the U.S. Department of State.

ALEXANDER R. VERSHBOW contributed to this volume as an associate editor of the 1980s Project at the Council on Foreign Relations. He has since become a Foreign Service Officer with the U.S. Department of State.

DATE DUE

NOV 7 1979	APR 3 1980
NOV 28 1979	T JUN 9 1982
DEC 19 1979	1982
CT OCT 16 1981	GR NOV 30 1982
CT NOV 16 1981	JT DEC 13 1985
CT DEC 7 1981	
CT DEC 30 1981	JT DEC 1985
GR JUL 6 1982	OCT 1986
H 30 /69 86	DEC 20 1994
CU OCT 05 1986	
OCT 22 1997	